FAITH IN CRISIS – HOW GOD SHOWS UP WHEN YOU NEED HIM MOST

Praise from Readers

In this gripping account a Christian doctor finds himself hostage in the American Embassy in Kuwait, a country he had come to serve. This true story reads like a suspense thriller. You won't want to put it down.
Tom Swift, Former Chair and Professor Emeritus,
Department of Neurology, Medical College of Georgia

This exciting account of captivity in the Middle East will draw you in, and you will not be able to put it down. This book's refreshing honesty about feelings of fear, depression, hopelessness, and the challenges of trusting God in uncertainty will boost your faith.
Laurie Myers, author, *The Shepherd's Song*, *The Lord is Their Shepherd*, and *Be Strong in the Lord*.

Jim and Shirley Carroll share their story of a lengthy and life-threatening politically enforced separation. Jim lives under tremendous physical and mental hardships with authentic questions and agonizing prayers. Shirley, who is stuck in the United States with their seven children, experiences God's faithfulness through His provision for their young family despite no income for months. Their experience changed them. Their

JIM AND SHIRLEY CARROLL

sharing it will change you. At times raw, but always real, this is a book you won't want to miss.

Ray and Jani Ortlund
Renewal Ministries https://ortlund.net

This story whets the appetite for the extraordinary world we can see when we walk by faith and not by sight.

George Robertson, PhD, Pastor, First Presbyterian Church, Augusta, Georgia

I believe this is a missionary classic. A must read. This is a look into the life of a missionary family living for the glory of God during uncertainty and difficult testing. What unfolds is the love story of Jim and Shirley, their seven children, and a faithful God. We encounter the raw emotions and doubts they go through while separated from each other. It shows us their oneness and trust for God to accomplish His glory in their ordeal. He does.

Phin Hitchcock, Fireside Ministries & Industries, Augusta, GA

I first heard Jim share his experience in the Kuwait embassy in 2009. I remember him concluding that time saying, "I'm embarrassed by how much God loves me." After reading this honest, startling account of his family's fight to trust in God's faithfulness through an extraordinarily difficult circumstance, you will no doubt echo his humility.

Nathan Wilson M.D., Missionary to Cusco, Peru,
Presidente, La Fuente Centro de Salud Integral

Once I started, I couldn't stop, so I spent an afternoon and finished the book. We had a child born in Yemen two months after Jim's release. This book helped me see how another family lived through the crisis. Even brief moments revealed to me the depth of

FAITH IN CRISIS

transparency throughout the book. Near the end, Shirley writes, "For too long a moment, I was mad at God for assuring me Jimmy would be there. My heart was pounding, and I was trying not to cry in front of the kids." Read the book. Walk with the Carrolls through a footnote in history where they help us with their raw feelings and faith questions. And to see God in their story.

Anonymous, Missionary in the Middle East

An incredible true-life story of resilience, determination, survival and faith, revealing with brutal honesty their prolonged daily struggle with uncertainty and worry, but all overcome by hope in the unfailing mercy and sovereignty of God. What Jim and Shirley Carroll have shared inspires courage to face our own crises with greater trust knowing that though we are weak, God is strong.

Drs. Ted and Sharon Kuhn, Co-Medical Directors for
Mission to the World

Dr. Jim Carroll's story of capture and eventual dramatic rescue is a powerful reminder our world is not governed by human forces and battles for political power. Jim and Shirley have given their lives to help people understand that through humility and service a person can change the world. My friendship and admiration has grown as I watched them for over twenty years live as humble servants believing that a grand human rescue is not only needed but is on the way.

Rev. Michael Hearon, Campus Outreach-National Leadership Team
First Presbyterian Church, Augusta, GA-Missions Pastor

FAITH IN CRISIS – HOW GOD SHOWS UP WHEN YOU NEED HIM MOST

JIM AND SHIRLEY CARROLL

CROSSLINK PUBLISHING

Faith in Crisis – How God Shows Up When You Need Him Most

CrossLink Publishing
www.crosslinkpublishing.com

Copyright, © 2016 Jim and Shirley Carroll

All rights reserved. No part of this book may be reproduced in any form, except for brief quotations in reviews, without the written permission of the author.

Printed in the United States of America. All rights reserved under International Copyright Law.

ISBN 978-1-63357-089-4

Library of Congress Control Number: 2016954445

Scripture quotations marked "ESV" are taken from The Holy Bible, English Standard Version. Copyright © 2000; 2001 by Crossway Bibles, a division of Good News Publishers. Used by permission. All rights reserved.

Table Of Contents

Foreword xi

Acknowledgements xiii

Introduction xv

Prologue xvii

Chapter 1 The Invasion 1

    Shirley 1

    Jim 3

Chapter 2 Shirley Waiting for Word 21

Chapter 3 Jim on the Run 35

Chapter 4 The Embassy August 18–24 51

    Jim 51

    Shirley 67

Chapter 5 Iraq Closes the Embassies 69

Chapter 6 Others Got Out, I Didn't 85

Chapter 7 One Month Anniversary and the Arab Roof 91

Chapter 8 Things Fall Apart 97

Chapter 9 Depression Sets In 105

Chapter 10 Pain, Self-Inflicted 113

Chapter 11 Fleas and Sand in the Tuna, Artillery at Night 119

Chapter 12 Happy Hour 127

Chapter 13 Bombing Is the Best News 133

Chapter 14 Shirley's Bubble 137

Chapter 15 More Evacuations, I'm Still Stuck 143

Chapter 16 The Well 147

Chapter 17 The Pullback That Never Happened 151

Chapter 18 Halloween, Pigeon Meat, God Only Wise,
and Kurt Vonnegut 157

Chapter 19 War Preparations 167

Chapter 20 Binary Weapons, Rania 173

Chapter 21 Thanksgiving 181

Chapter 22 Shirley to the Rescue 189

Chapter 23 Release and Reception 193

    Jim 193

    Shirley 198

Epilogue 201

The Authors 203

Acknowledgements

More than twenty-five years have elapsed since the Iraqi invasion of Kuwait and our involvement in that crisis. Thanks to urging of family and friends, we finally got the courage to write the story.

Many of those who helped us during the trial are mentioned by name in the memoir. The others—and they were countless: neighbors, church members, friends from the Medical College of Georgia—provided money and food, whatever we needed. They were reflections of God's mercy.

We give thanks to David Aretha for his developmental edits of the book, and also for his encouragement.

The text in this book was compiled from our recollections, the diaries we kept, and from various historical records, such as *Strangers When We Met – A Century of American Community in Kuwait, Siege - Crisis Leadership: The Survival of U.S. Kuwait Embassy*, both by Nathaniel Howell, and *Days of Fear, The Inside Story of the Iraqi Invasion and Occupation of Kuwait* by John Levins. Some names, locations, and identifying characteristics have been changed to protect the privacy of those depicted. Dialogue was recreated from memory.

Introduction

On August 2, 1990, Iraq invaded the little Persian Gulf country of Kuwait, resulting in the longest siege of a US embassy in American history. Jim and Shirley Carroll were tent-making missionaries in the country. Jim was trapped in the embassy while Shirley, home on leave with their seven children, languished in Augusta, Georgia, with no means of support. This is the story of their walk by faith through those difficult days and how the Lord preserved them.

Prologue

"For we walk by faith, not by sight." (*English Standard Version*, 2 Corinthians 5:7).

There are two ways to walk by faith.

One is the path you know. The other path is the mystery. The paths are the same.

I'm just waking up. The sheet is light on my skin, and I pull it up around my shoulders for warmth. The breeze blowing over me is fresh and cool. I stretch my back and anticipate the day working with the students on the children's ward at Mubarak Hospital by Kuwait University Medical School. But why is there a breeze? There's no breeze in our house.

Now I'm awake, startled by the presence of the breeze, and I remember: there will be no day at Mubarak with the med students. I'm outside and the moist wind that smells like the sea covers me as it comes in off the Persian Gulf. The temperature is pleasant enough for a mid-September early morning in Kuwait. I'm on top of a white three-story building, and my mattress is lying directly on the roof. My friend Joe is over on the other side of the building snoring away.

JIM AND SHIRLEY CARROLL

I drag myself up from the mattress on the roof's hard surface, turn, and walk forward to the three-foot retaining wall. The blue-gray Gulf is 300 yards to the east extending out to the horizon, and the sun is ready to rise. The building where I slept is one of several inside a giant tankproof white wall topped with razor wire.

No fishing boats are out in the Gulf where they should be this time of day. I see four pitiful Iraqi soldiers walking in two pairs outside the compound wall. They have only sandals, no boots or socks, and their uniforms aren't identical like they should be for soldiers. They look like they've been pulled from the streets of Baghdad. They're flipping their rifles around as if they don't really care about being on guard duty.

I'm not supposed to be here at the embassy. I'm a doctor, a pediatric neurologist, and I have no business here. I should be with my family, maybe back in the US, at least back at the hospital with patients and students here in Kuwait. But here I am in the US embassy in Kuwait, and the diplomats tell us we can't leave. I believe them. Iraqi soldiers who never smile surround us.

Why am I here? This kind of thing is only in the movies. What's going to happen next? But more important, how did this happen to me?

Chapter 1

The Invasion

August 1 – Shirley

Our five-bedroom Hilton Head Island style house with its cedar siding and surrounding porches had provided a brief refuge from the desert, but we were looking forward to departing Augusta, Georgia, and our return to Kuwait. The greenery and huge trees in the neighborhood was still startling to me after living in the dry, yellow-brown colors of the desert. Nevertheless, I had begun to miss even the sandy dust that invaded our Kuwait home on a daily basis. But the news of the day was a concern.

Jim had already returned to Kuwait after spending his early summer break in the States. Kuwait University, where Jimmy was employed, had given us tickets to fly to the US during the summer months. This was a part of Jim's employment agreement.

We were thankful for the respite from the summer weather in Kuwait, where daytime temperature reaches 120–130 degrees. Anyone who can be out of Kuwait during its summer definitely

JIM AND SHIRLEY CARROLL

wants to be anywhere else. We were packed and had our return tickets ready to go back to Kuwait in two weeks. We had stayed in Augusta to complete one of Matthew's many plastic surgeries on his birthmarks. That stage of the surgery was over, and we were ready to head back to Kuwait. Everything was prepared, and the six of our seven children, ranging from two to fourteen, who were to return with me, were excited about seeing their dad after nearly two months.

I had a friend over for dinner, iced sweet tea, vegetable soup and salad, and afterwards we prayed together. "Lord, please provide a husband for Elaine. We trust in your wisdom and know you'll do what's best. She wants your best and desires a husband and we ask you to answer her request. We love you and know you're a God we can trust." Almost forty, Elaine wanted a husband while she could still have children.

Elaine prayed for our family. "I pray Shirley and the children will have safe travel back to Kuwait. I pray for their mission work with the Kuwaitis, and most for the Bedouins, that they would come to know you. I ask that their house will get rented before she leaves." Although I had already rented the house for the year, the party had just backed out of the deal. It was a mess. How was I going to have time to rent the house before we left for Kuwait? Elaine continued. "I ask that Shirley and the children will rely only on you in their mission to Kuwait. Lord, please bless them in their work with the people there. We trust in you."

As we were praying the phone rang. Jimmy was making his regular check-in call from Kuwait, but I jumped into the conversation first. "The news here says Iraq is on the border of Kuwait about to invade the country. The news is really alarming to me, Jimmy. It sounds like the Iraqis really mean it." The matter had been boiling for weeks, but we had hoped for the best. The trouble, we thought, was old news, another squabble between Arab brothers, nothing more than the standard fare for that part of the world.

FAITH IN CRISIS

Kuwait was seven hours ahead, and Jimmy was there at our home late in the evening getting ready to watch the local news on TV. I continued on my concern. "CNN here in the US says the Iraqis are about to invade Kuwait. What's happening there? What do you think? Maybe you should get a plane back to the States. It really looks serious. I don't want you there in Kuwait by yourself."

"Absolutely not. I'm not panicking over this and jumping on a plane. Nothing's going on here in Kuwait. The country's quiet and there's no bad news here. Nobody is even mentioning the Iraqis. I can't leave anyway. I just turned in my passport to get our residency permits renewed." He was stuck, and he gave one more disturbing report. "For some reason, my paycheck is delayed this month. Don't worry about it. It'll come soon."

I knew he wouldn't budge. He had that tone. The rest of the conversation was more pleasant, and we were anxious to see each other in a few days. By the way, the check never came.

###

August 1–2 – Jim

I had been out on the street downtown shopping for a new TV. I had never seen the city so quiet.

Kuwait City, near the center of Kuwait on the coast, is the only population center of the little country tucked in the northwestern corner of the Persian Gulf between Iran and Iraq to the north and Saudi Arabia to the south. The maximum dimensions of Kuwait are 125 miles north to south and 100 miles east to west.

In 1990 more than half the population of two million was comprised of expatriates who were in the country as workers. Some were Westerners like us, but the greater number were laborers from the developing world. From the look of the streets on that hot August day, most were either out of the country during the summer heat or remaining in their homes.

3

JIM AND SHIRLEY CARROLL

After I drove back to our home in the Jabriya section of the city, and following Shirley's call, I switched on the news. The August 1, 1990 report on the evening TV was even blander than it had been on preceding days, and I should have been suspicious. The Ministry of Information Station, KTV-2, was known for its commitment to boring news, often featuring videos of the emir greeting his guests of the day, and that evening the station was at its tedious best. The young Kuwaiti woman with no hair covering and the British accent said, "Kuwaiti and Iraqi ministers continue to discuss grievances in the quiet setting of Jeddah. Hosni Mubarak, mediating the conference on behalf of the Arab League, remains confident in a peaceful resolution." There was no mention of troop deployments or any intention of hostilities. Kuwait was safe.

But what the Kuwait TV gal didn't say was that the problem was a big deal. It was a giant cat against a little mouse. Iraq had brought financial and social disaster on itself during its eight-year war with Iran, a war neither side could win. Iran had sent waves of soldiers, some children, to be massacred by Iraqi artillery. One of my friends in the Kuwaiti military told me about the battle of Al-Faw. "The sharks below Bubiyan Island at the outflow of the Shatt Al-Arab had a picnic on the blood and body parts floating out from the fight." Both sides were scarred by the war and Saddam wanted to recoup his financial loses. The soldiers he lost—never mind.

Tiny, rich Kuwait with one of the world's highest per capita incomes had supported their northern Arab neighbor, loaning the Iraqis nearly twenty billion dollars to support the war effort. The Iraqis didn't want to pay it back, maybe they couldn't, and they wanted the northern Kuwaiti oil fields, perhaps as far south as Mutla Ridge, the highest point in Kuwait. Mutla was the rocky escarpment north of the city running parallel to the Subiya Motorway. Kuwait was the obvious solution to Saddam's money problem.

FAITH IN CRISIS

The Iraqis had accused the Kuwaitis of "slant drilling," meaning the Kuwait drillers aimed their oilrig drills under the border and into Iraqi oilfields in order to steal Iraq's main source of revenue. The allegation had no foundation. But Iraq said it was all their land anyway based on old maps, which existed prior to the British redrawing the map of the Middle East. All these claims had been in the news for months, and there was nothing new in the demands. We knew the Iraqis just wanted more oil to fatten up their depleted coffers. Kuwait had been an independent state for years, and there was no basis for any of the Iraqi demands.

But the two sides were talking and making progress, at least that's what the news lady said. In fact by the time of the news broadcast, we later learned the peace conference had pretty much dissolved.

A week earlier, the emir had offered his own poetic description of the negotiations, a "Summer Cloud." A summer cloud in Kuwait has no antecedent and no consequence. There is no rain before it and none after. Thus, the remark was designed to reassure the populace, at least the small number who remained in Kuwait during the summer heat. The emir had said all was well in Kuwait. I had no reason, other than Shirley's concerning comments that evening, to worry about Saddam.

And I had even convinced Shirley of the peace of Kuwait. "Well, okay, Jimmy, I guess we'll see you soon at the airport in Kuwait."

At 2:00 AM the first explosions began, and I woke up. Because of Shirley's warning I hadn't slept well anyway, and as soon as the jets roared over the city, I knew. Commercial jets never sounded like that, and they never flew so low over the city. All the explosions were in the distance at first, but they were repeated with only brief interruptions. The booms moved closer to our home.

I looked outside in the street and at the nearby houses, and there was no movement. A few lights were on in the homes of my neighbors across the street. Usually they would be dark at this hour.

Small arms fire erupted in a nearby neighborhood, and there was no more sleep. From hearing TV shows with simulated automatic weapons fire, I recognized the distinctive pop-pop sounds of an automatic assault rifle. We later confirmed from arms experts that these were AK-47s, perhaps from the Russians or from US commercial arms dealers. We never learned who was shooting.

At 6:00 AM, Alina, my Sudanese lab assistant, phoned. She was abrupt: "Doctor, don't go outside." It was just getting light, and sporadic artillery fire continued in the distance.

For some strange reason, I couldn't resist a silly response. "Why not?"

"Doctor, there is war!" I took comfort in the fact she cared enough to call me. I didn't even know she had my phone number. But in Kuwait such information, almost any personal data, makes its passage among those who wanted to know.

I mumbled crazy stuff, nothing of any consequence, a disorganized response. What was the appropriate response to *there is war*? I was scared but tried not show it. She had given her advice, I had none for her, and we closed. "Take care, Alina." I never saw her again, and I hope she made it out of Kuwait safely. Sudan supported Iraq, so I suppose she was okay. The invaders favored those Kuwait residents whose countries came out in support of Iraq.

For the moment our large villa in the Jabriya section of the city was my fortress. The university had provided a three-story "green villa" for Shirley and me and our seven children. It was referred to as one of the "green villas" because of the color of the outside tile siding, identical to the other university-sponsored houses on the block. We were the only Americans living in the area. I heard no more firing near our home, just booms in the distance. As near as I could tell, the Iraqis weren't blowing up large areas. The jets had stopped flying over our zone. I had no way of determining the extent of the fighting and even whether

FAITH IN CRISIS

or not there was a full-scale invasion. Maybe the Iraqis were just probing Kuwait and trying to frighten the government into paying ransom for protection. Although Kuwait had every right to its own sovereignty, they couldn't fend off the Iraqi behemoth.

At seven in the morning, my friend Haddad, a medical school faculty colleague who lived in the villa near our home, knocked on my door. His food-spotted white shirt was open at the collar, as usual, his gray chest hair overflowing the top button. Haddad was a portly, always informally-dressed man, longtime Kuwait resident but a Jordanian married to a Kuwaiti. "Jim, we need to talk. I think Iraq has invaded." He smelled of alcohol, a bit early in the day, but I couldn't blame him.

I recalled our first meeting when I had come over to visit Kuwait. He had taken me out for dinner and brought a brown bag containing whiskey. Alcohol was illegal in Kuwait and he thought that I, as an American, needed alcohol with dinner. On that occasion I had disappointed him. But now with a possible invading army, I cast no fault.

We tried the TV, but there was nothing but fuzz and static. We had no source of information other than what we saw and heard, which was minimal. My own picture of what an invasion should look like had not been fulfilled. I had not seen a soldier or a tank, no devastation of buildings, no plumes of smoke, only the gunfire and sounds of artillery far off in the distance.

Had the Iraqis really invaded? Our defensive hope continued to be that the Iraqis were just trying to scare the Kuwaitis into giving up some oil or money. Nothing decisive had happened as far as we could determine.

From my house, Haddad phoned his contacts around town, and most knew less than we did. Some didn't answer, which was worrisome at the early hour. No, there weren't any definite reports, just spotty accounts of what others had told them. Yes, some Iraqi troops had come across the border, but where were they? Was it just a token force or a real invasion? Our snapshots of the invasion provided only circumstantial information.

Haddad asked me over to his home. I definitely wanted company, so I followed. While his wife fixed eggs and coffee, the phone rang and Haddad answered. "Yes, I see. I understand. It must be true." He looked at me nodding and gesturing with an upward motion of his left hand. He was dramatic in his seriousness, but then Haddad was always theatrical so I didn't rely on his gestures. He hung up the phone. "Jim, three wounded soldiers were brought into the Casualty Department." Truth or rumors multiplied fast between Haddad and me, and I learned how war stories were born. Perhaps there had been a full-scale invasion.

But if so, why weren't we seeing more evidence of the offensive? Haddad's last experience in an invasion was the Israeli takeover of Palestine in 1948, where the Israelis had been more efficient than the Iraqis. "This is nothing like what Israel did to us." I'd heard the account many times from Haddad, and he still resented the Jews taking his beloved homeland from him and his family. He went back to the story when he was anxious or angry at uncertainty. And we were in that mode, both of us hypervigilant, waiting for more data.

Then a series of detonations began to occur several hundred feet in the air above our neighborhood. We ducked our heads with each explosion. The blasts had no obvious military purpose other than perhaps to frighten civilians. The plan worked with me. A few pieces of debris from the discharges struck our villas, but there was no damage. I could hear the debris cluttering down on the roof.

If it was war, then there would be more than three soldiers wounded at Mubarak. I was concerned about our responsibility. "Should we go over to Mubarak?" Mubarak Al-Kabeer (Mubarak the Great) Hospital near our home in the Jabriya area of Kuwait City was one of several state-supported facilities in Kuwait. The hospital had been named after Mubarak Al-Sabah, who came to power at the end of the nineteenth century after murdering his two half-brothers. After negotiating a beneficial treaty with the British, he was honored and regarded as the founder of modern Kuwait.

I answered my own query. "I suppose we have to go." If not, we would have just stayed in our homes wondering about our duty. "Let's get it over with." There was no shooting except for an occasional explosion in the distance, so Haddad and I decided to venture out. As pediatricians we were still doctors, and we felt a reluctant sense of duty. We headed back behind Haddad's house to Mubarak.

The red facade hospital with white trim was only a block from our homes, so we traipsed across the vacant parking lot and up the two flights of stairs to the pediatric floor. The elevator wasn't functional, which was not unusual. Haddad was panting as we reached the floor. Most of the doctors hadn't made it in, a bad sign, and none of the female doctors had arrived. The cleaning staff, which usually worked early in the day, was nowhere to be seen.

There was no action on the pediatric floor. Usually it was full of commotion at that hour. We then went back to the first floor and the casualty department, where there was total confusion with wounded Kuwaiti soldiers. The few doctors and nurses present were going from room to room. We walked around the area, and the surgeons and a few nurses were attending to the needs. Haddad and I were pretty helpless in that venue. We looked at each other but didn't speak about our lack of utility.

About 11:00 AM ten Iraqi helicopters circled the hospital but didn't land. From the third floor of the hospital, the children's floor, I watched soldiers firing at each other around the corner of the medical school across the street. Their uniforms were similar, and I couldn't tell Kuwaitis from Iraqis. No soldiers fell. How could they fire so many bullets and not hit anything?

I had no understanding of how a country was invaded and taken over. Either they're here or they're not. Right? As far as

JIM AND SHIRLEY CARROLL

I could determine from our vantage point, there was limited conflict. We soon learned invasions don't happen with everything taken over at once. Invasions are piecemeal, incremental, parts of the city and country taken over bit by bit, groups of soldiers sent here and some sent there. Any consolidation of control took time. What we saw that morning were early fragments of the invasion. It was confusion rather than stabilization or pacification. Would the invading Iraqi soldiers know who to shoot and who to let pass? Would they have sufficient discipline to refrain from shooting civilians?

Haddad and I were lost about what to do next. "What do you think, Jim? What should we do here?" Kuwait was his home and I was an outsider, and he was asking me.

"I have no idea. Let's just stay put for a while."

We had no inkling of a plan. Was the Iraqi incursion temporary? Maybe things would return to normal. The Iraqis would get what they want, and tomorrow they would be gone. Should we remain at the hospital and see what we could do there? Kuwaiti soldier casualties were arriving but the number was small, and our pediatric services were not needed for them.

There were few pediatric patients. Many families were either outside Kuwait for the summer or afraid to bring their children to the hospital for all but the most serious illnesses. The July and August temperatures approaching 130°F sent many Kuwaitis and expatriates on holiday. With the news of the invasion, the female physicians were afraid to leave their homes. Was it safe for us to be there? But as the head of the pediatric unit for the summer it was my responsibility to be there, and there were no Iraqis occupying the hospital.

We stalled around on the hospital ward for a while. "Haddad, there's just nothing we can do. But I hate not to be here." He nodded and looked down, his hands in his pants pockets. It was a posture of surrender.

FAITH IN CRISIS

There were not as many casualties as it had initially appeared, and there was nothing for us to do as pediatricians. We waited until there had been no gunfire for a while in the vicinity, and then we walked back across the car park to Haddad's home where his wife fixed us a meal with cold cuts and salad.

His children looked puzzled. Both were teenagers and able to understand as much as we were. The older boy, Abdullah, said to his dad, "What will happen to our school? I want to see my friends today and see if they're okay." Everyone was focused on himself, me included.

I went back to my house, tried the phone, and found the line working. The long distance line couldn't be intact but I tried it anyway. Shirley picked up the phone.

"Jimmy?"

"Yes, it's me. I think the Iraqis are taking over."

"It's all over CNN. Kuwait's been captured. They're defeated. Jimmy, can you come home?" Just then there was a tremendous explosion, one I could hear from my house, and the line went dead. I figured the Iraqis had blown up the international connection center. I tried to place the call again. Nothing, even though the local lines were still open.

Yes, I had to get out, and I should have heeded Shirley's earlier advice. If I had gone to the airport before the Iraqis attacked, I might have made it. I phoned my jovial, balding Lebanese friend, Abbas, who worked at Kuwait Airways. He'd helped me many times with flights for my family and me, and I had his home phone number.

"Abbas, this is Doctor Jim, can you get me a flight to the US?"

"Doctor, the Iraqis have taken the airport. There's no more Kuwait Airways." He was more frightened than I was. "We all must stay inside. Doctor, can't you hear the gunfire? I must stay here at home with my wife and children."

Less than one day into the invasion and I was a coward making a senseless call to a man who couldn't help me. He couldn't help himself or his family.

August 4

Haddad and I made another guilt-fed trip to the hospital. Other Kuwaiti soldiers, their faces gaunt and unsmiling, began to come to the hospital, shed their uniforms, and put on patient gowns. As if a hospital gown would protect them if the Iraqis came. We heard some Kuwaiti armed forces units had fought bravely, but others had not. We had no reason to think any news we received was accurate, but it was certain the Kuwaiti troops had been overwhelmed. Iraq's army was the fourth largest in the world, with half a million soldiers. The Kuwaiti armed forces numbered 20,000, and some were not even Kuwaiti citizens.

Kuwaiti soldiers who were not wounded began to collect in the hospital corridors and patient rooms. They had hidden their uniforms and donned the pale blue patient gowns. They kept their weapons, and they were taking refuge in the hospital as patients with rifles. We were afraid the Iraqis would discover them and a firefight would ensue inside the hospital. The doctors and nurses, those who remained, were scared and furious at the soldiers. The Indian nurse on the floor screamed, "You cowards get out of here and fight!"

The hospital administrator showed up on the scene and confronted the nightgowned soldiers. "You're going to get us shot. What will you do if the Iraqis come? Fight them here in hall? You don't look like patients. You'll not fool anyone." Somehow the administrator persuaded them either to put down their weapons and assume full patient status or get out. Most chose the former. They succeeded only in looking like soldiers in pajamas, and the risk of their presence persisted.

August 5

Haddad and I continued to attend the hospital, but there was little for us to do. Faisal, another pediatrician from the Faculty of Medicine, was there, too. Faisal was more diligent and intense, and he had taken over the pediatric floor. He remained uncommunicative with Haddad and me, and he busied himself with the remaining patients, looking more serious each hour. His own situation, as a Palestinian married to a Kuwaiti, was ambiguous. The Palestinian Liberation Organization under Yasser Arafat had sided with Saddam.

None of the female physicians had shown up, and we decided they probably wouldn't. Most had called in and informed us their families forbade them to venture out. The streets were too dangerous for them to travel in their cars. The culture dictated women should be risk-averse in even the safest circumstance, and we were in the opposite of 'safe.' Rapes by invading soldiers were already reported in the community.

What was our status during the invasion as non-soldiers? What does an invading army do to regular citizens? And I wasn't a "regular citizen." I was an American. Was I a prize? There was no answer yet to the Iraqi plan for Americans.

Haddad and I decided to walk over to the medical school, which was only half a block away. We hadn't been there yet, and we wanted to see the condition of the offices.

As we exited the hospital and turned left up the road off the hospital porch, we saw them. There were about fifty soldiers posted in single lines on each side of the roadway between the hospital and medical school. They were at attention with their rifles at their right sides, left arm behind their backs, rifle butts resting on the pavement and the barrel supported in their right hand. They looked straight ahead, trying not to pay attention to us. Great! Kuwaiti soldiers were here protecting the hospital.

But wait—they were not Kuwaiti. They were Iraqi. Haddad and I figured out the truth about the same time, and he whispered, "Don't look at them, just keep walking." What else could we do? Somehow we kept our cool and continued walking between the rows of soldiers. We had on our white doctor coats on and our stethoscopes around our necks, what we had deemed as our safety costumes. They identified us as noncombatants (boy, were we noncombatants!) and doctors who might be of some value to them. The soldiers were stiff and disciplined, and we wondered if they were Republican Guard unit, Saddam's crack troops.

The medical school had so far been untouched. The security guard at the entrance was there as usual, looking puzzled about his role. Why in the world had he reported for work? He was not a Kuwaiti citizen, and apparently he still thought he had a job. He knew us and nodded as we entered, apparently thankful to see some semblance of normality. We walked across the marble floor of the high-ceiled rotunda, climbed up the flights to our offices—which had remained untouched—picked up some journals, any journal just for show to prove we had a purpose in our journey, put them under our arm, and walked the gauntlet back to Mubarak. My friends had told me I could pass for Palestinian with my long face, generous nose, and darker skin than the average white American. So I suppose that was a temporary positive. The thought began to occur to me: *Was I a potential hostage?*

We saw no signs of aggression, no indications of battle.

Haddad and I went back to the third floor of Mubarak and collapsed in the doctors' small workroom, not knowing what to do next. Haddad said, "Let me fix you a Nescafe." The grainy coffee-colored crystals were placed in a cup and hot water poured over them. This was the hospital excuse for coffee, but it tasted so good.

Then we heard gunfire outside in the courtyard. We looked out the window trying to be careful not to expose ourselves to the stray bullets. A Kuwaiti soldier in a pale blue hospital gown, his

FAITH IN CRISIS

buttocks barely covered by the robe, was running about with a machine gun in his arms. He ran from place to place trying to hide. Soon several Iraqi soldiers appeared just behind him. There were more shots, but no one was hit. How could they keep missing with automatic weapons? Then the Kuwaiti and the Iraqis disappeared around the corner of the hospital, and we saw and heard nothing more of them.

Shortly afterward, the Kuwaiti hospital administrator convinced the blue-gowned soldiers to renounce their status as patients and leave the hospital.

It was clear the Iraqis would eventually occupy the hospital. They had already moved in around the hospital and their incursion was a certainty. They would need the facility for their own wounded. There was more pressure on me about my status as an American. I acknowledged my value as a potential target, and Haddad was concerned about me. "I think you'd better be careful about coming to the hospital. We don't know what the Iraqis will do to Americans." We had no indication yet the Iraqis bore ill will against Americans, and I wanted to think they did not. The US had supported Iraq during their 1980–1988 war with Iran.

"But I'm supposed to be here." My statement bore little enthusiasm. Somehow I had been appointed head of the pediatric unit before the invasion. I looked around the ward where there were few children. Just based on the need, Haddad was right. They didn't need me to care for the small number of pediatric patients, and I should get out while there was still time. My token bravery was useless.

I looked over in the corner near the window of the children's ward. Three-and-a-half-year-old Rania was there trying to stand in her big crib with the bars and the net on top. Paralyzed on her right side, it was hard for her to rise. She smiled at me and waved with her left hand.

JIM AND SHIRLEY CARROLL

Rania was the smaller of twins born to a poor Palestinian family. She was born prematurely, and they had left her at Maternity Hospital even after she was discharged. They couldn't manage all their six children as it was. The hospital authorities located the family, and the police forced them to take her home. Rania was the focus of their frustration and anger over their poverty. The concept of the battered child was not well recognized in Kuwait at that time, and the violence had proceeded. Most Kuwaiti physicians said, "The battered child syndrome does not exist in Kuwait." It was a matter of Arab pride. But of course it did occur, just as it does the world over. Rania was a prime example. It was uncertain who was guilty, the father or the mother. A battered child with brain damage, Rania often ended up in the Mubarak with fresh abuse.

Our son, Peter, had attached himself to Rania, and often went over to the hospital to assist with her physical therapy. We had taken her into our home over the preceding months, and there had been little opposition to our keeping her. She lived with us as a sort of foster child, no problem as long as the legalities weren't challenged. The hospital had even given us a paper with an official-looking stamp indicating it was legal for us to keep her with us. Every paper in the Arab world must have a stamp. And the parents were happy to be rid of her. We wanted to adopt her but since we were not Muslim, there was no way. No stamp could fix that. With Shirley's departure back to the US for the summer, she had to go back to her family.

She was back in the hospital with more injuries, and now it wasn't safe for me to be in the hospital. This was the last time I saw Rania. Her image stuck in my mind: the sun streaming through the window by her crib, the light bouncing off the dust particles in the air creating visible angles from the sun's rays, out the window behind her an Iraqi helicopter gunship hovering over the hospital grounds, Rania laughing and waving at me with the arm that was not paralyzed.

My thoughts about Rania had interrupted my concentration on Haddad's remarks. "We can take care of the hospital, Jim. It's too risky for you. You better stay away. They'll know right away you're an American." Haddad was an Arab physician, one with Palestinian connections, and the Iraqis would probably be happy to have him on board at the hospital. He might even be considered an ally. While I could be mistaken for a pale Arab, they would know as soon as I opened my mouth with my fragmentary, Southern US-accented Arabic.

I walked back to my house, where I supposed I might be safe. There on the roadway in front of our home were two spent cartridges. The larger shell casing had a stamp on the bottom, which read L2A2 83 POF. Vigilant for details, I wrote down the information. I couldn't read the bottom of the smaller cartridge. I later learned POF stood for Pakistani Ordinance Factory. So Pakistan sold ammo to the Iraqis.

I didn't know there had been gunfire in my neighborhood, but the shell casings indicated its presence. When had the gunfire occurred? Had I slept through it? But it was starting to be dangerous for Iraqi sentries after dark. The Kuwaiti resistance was beginning to form, and the poor, lone Iraqi on duty was an easy target. If it was risky for them, what was the risk for me? Iraqi patrols in jeeps had begun to drive through the neighborhood at night enforcing the curfew. The spent cartridge shells were proof of military activity in front of my house.

I recalled our street had been the site of another sort of violence earlier in the year, one that was acceptable in the culture. The family occupying the house next to Haddad had tethered a young camel by the light post. They fed and watered the animal daily for several weeks. We thought, as did our children, that the camel was a pet. The animal was docile and uncomplaining.

Then, there was the day when we all returned from a shopping trip and saw the camel stretched out partially in the street and partially on the curb. There was still some movement from the animal, but blood was flowing from its carotid artery and jugular vein into the street drain. Shirley and I struggled to explain that the animal had been killed as meat for a celebration. The method of slaughter was *halal*, meaning legal according to Islamic law due to the method of slaughter.

Thus, everything was still new to us in Kuwait, preparing to eat a pet for dinner, and now one Arab neighbor attacking another. I couldn't calibrate.

This had been a strange invasion. The electricity and water remained intact. Our home air conditioner continued to function. Though most stores were closed, food was still available in some of the markets. I had no idea about the course of events or what should be expected, and the invasion didn't yet seem real. But my invasion experience was limited to one.

August 6

I was confused, frightened, and uncertain what to do next. But the worst emotion was the anxiety—not knowing what would happen next. I fixated on my need for knowing, which for the period of the invasion would have no endpoint. The only solution seemed to be some sort of conflagration, something dramatic enough to bring about a conclusion. I could see no good conflagration.

I started journaling. The act of writing was a way to dissipate pent-up anxiety. All my journal notes were to Shirley. If I didn't get out of this alive, perhaps she could read these. Some excerpts from the day: *fifth day of the invasion – I pray for you constantly – Over the last day or two, I have developed a real trust you will triumph over this in a victorious way – I have learned something very important – I'm not afraid to die – This is a great gift – a man could live all his life and not know this – My worst fear is that I will be taken hostage – I thought we might leave Kuwait for good next year, but God wasn't finished with us. I see a little of the plan now. I'm not giving up. I'll try with my last breath to return to you even though I'm trapped by an invading army– You're a woman who walks by faith – I trust your judgment with all the decisions you'll have to make without me. The waiting is really bad. I've been going here and there to stay with friends, in order not to develop a pattern or attract attention. I pray I'm able to give you this journal in person. Love, Jimmy*

My fear of hostage status dominated the following days.

For the first two days, the hospital had seen some action, but the flow of patients plummeted and there wasn't much to do. As yet, I didn't know if the Iraqis were taking Western hostages, but the potential seemed clear to me. And of course, I recalled the 1979 Iranian hostage crisis. I decided to take Haddad's advice. I stopped going to the hospital in order not to expose myself to the Iraqis.

Chapter 2

Shirley Waiting for Word: August 7–August 18

We heard nothing more from Jim. Had he tried to leave with our Bedouin friends who lived in Ahmadi? Surely he would turn to them first. I kept expecting a call from somewhere in Saudi Arabia or Jordan, but there was nothing—nothing for weeks.

The Iraqi invasion was all over the news. As Kuwait was seven hours ahead of our time, I got up at one or two in the morning to hear the reports that were relentless on CNN. Our TV was on constantly, and we learned all about the military action, more than I needed to know. Our friends bombarded me with the information I already knew. But there was nothing about Jimmy.

How had this all come together? My grandmother, a widow barely making it financially, reared me from infancy. She forfeited her life for me, sent me to a private girls' school, and provided the secure home I would never have had without her. My grandmother was my life example of true sacrifice. I worked all through high school and college and, with scholarships, graduated from the University of Louisville.

For Jim, it had been the opposite. He admitted he was a child of privilege. An only child born to older parents, his mom and dad doted on his intellectual abilities and gave him everything he wanted. In order to provide him the best school opportunity, they moved from the little town of Eminence, Kentucky, to Louisville when he was twelve. He started college after his junior year of high school, and he was off. Jim completed his college work in two years and began medical school at twenty.

Before Jim and I got married, we talked about going to Africa as missionaries. We thought we could do anything. Together we remembered the stories of Schweitzer, his Lambarene mission hospital in Gabon, and his winning the Nobel Peace prize in 1952 for his work. We weren't aware Schweitzer had denied the divinity of Jesus in his classic work, *The Quest of the Historical Jesus*. We were consumed by the romance and idealism of the time, not the reality.

On our wedding bands, we inscribed phrases from the last verse of Robert Frost's poem, *Stopping by Woods on a Snowy Evening*. The poem, by President Kennedy's inaugural poet, emphasized promises and keeping one's personal responsibilities. And such was our mantra.

After we got married in 1967, I completed my masters in sociology and worked as a community organizer in downtown Louisville during the riots in the spring of 1968. I felt I had been inaugurated into action when the bullets came whizzing around me as I hunkered down behind the church altar. Such were our experiences, dreams and talks in the heroic, idealistic sixties. We thought we could we do it all. No—that's not right: *we were sure of it*. We wanted to do some great thing. These were the days of "Abraham, Martin and John." (Dion, 1968, YouTube).

FAITH IN CRISIS

Our knowledge of missions was sorely limited, however. And after our marriage, life became busier and more harried than we ever thought.

In 1969 we had one natural child, John, while we lived in Louisville, but I was unable to get pregnant again for years even though we wanted more children. Jimmy did two years in the Navy and went on to a three-year residency in Colorado and then another fellowship and a faculty post at Washington University in St Louis. We decided to adopt a child, Peter, just before St. Louis. And then after we moved to St. Louis, we adopted a child from Korea, Ruth. I became pregnant fourteen years after our first natural child, and our fourth child, Rebecca, was born. We moved on to Augusta, Georgia, in 1984 and a new faculty position there for Jim at the medical school. He had become enveloped in academic medicine, and our missions' plan was defunct for the moment.

In Augusta we joined the First Presbyterian Church, which was strongly evangelistic and missions-oriented, another big change and awakening for us. We finally really began to learn about missions. Schweitzer slipped into the background, and Jim and Elizabeth Elliot with her *Through Gates of Splendor* came to the foreground, along with *Bruchko* and *Peace Child*, and all the other stories of great warriors of the faith who honored Jesus as Lord.

I became pregnant again with Timothy, and very nearly at the same time we adopted another baby from Korea, Matthew—number six. There was no way we could have or would have had all those children on our own plan. But we loved God's plan.

And I became pregnant again: Lydia—number seven. With great gratitude toward God for his blessings to us, his mercy and his grace, I was filled with a deep desire to obey him in whatever way I could.

Jeremiah 29:11–13 spoke to me: "For I know the plans that I have for you, declares the Lord, plans for welfare and not for evil, to give you a future and a hope. Then you will call upon me and come and pray to me, and I will hear you. You will seek me and find me, when you search for me with all your heart."

Jim felt God calling us to missions overseas and directly to missions with Muslims. We took classes through Columbia Bible College that we hoped would prepare us. We went with a mission board directed to Muslim church planting. Then, a job possibility for Jim developed at Kuwait University medical school. Since we could not enter a Muslim country as stated missionaries, we needed a reason to work in the country. The job opening provided the platform required for us to enter the country. God seemed to be opening the way for us, and we went with the design we saw in front of us. All the planning came together fast, maybe too fast, and in 1988 we departed for Kuwait along with our seven children. We tried to sell our house in Augusta but couldn't, and we therefore rented our house for the time we were in Kuwait.

We weren't nearly ready for the cultural surprises we experienced in Kuwait. I tried very hard to learn Arabic and took classes at local language school, but I was never able to really communicate in Arabic other than simple greetings. This was certainly a barrier in my trying to form relationships with the people.

I was totally unprepared for life in Kuwait when we first got there. I didn't know the language, nor did I know how to go to the grocery. I didn't know what a local grocery market, often called a coop, looked like. I did not even know how to get food for the children. I had taken a double stroller for our two small boys but didn't realize that you can't push a stroller in the sand.

We had car seats for all the children in the US, but in Kuwait we learned no one used car seats. And the car we initially rented was not large enough for car seats for the children. As a mom I thought you couldn't travel around with children without car seats, but I soon realized along with this and everything else that our trust just had to be in the Lord in all the circumstances. I couldn't control anything.

FAITH IN CRISIS

Another member of our mission team prepared the way for Jim, the children, and me to go into the desert and visit the Bedouins. Through these contacts we were introduced to this people group on the fringe of rich Kuwaiti society. These proud, independent people viewed their own culture and way of life as the best. By our desire to be with them, we honored them. The children and I drove into the desert several times a week during the day in order to fellowship with the Bedouin women and children. The women and children visited separately from the men, so Jimmy often called on the men alone.

Jimmy drove to their home with us in the evenings—but we divided up upon arrival—and he sat with the men in their greeting area, which had a thick carpet and pillows on the floor, no chairs. Sometimes Peter, who was then twelve, accompanied him rather than the children and me.

Our children, of course, were unable to speak Arabic, but it didn't seem to be a problem for them. Although my verbal communication was limited, a bond formed with the women, and particularly with Um Salem (mother of Salem), the senior woman of clan. The fact I was breastfeeding Lydia along with their breastfeeding their children seemed to connect us together.

Our children were unable to function in the school in Kuwait since they didn't know Arabic. As I had taken homeschool materials with us, we quickly turned to that model. Homeschooling fit in well with the plan because we could plan our visits to the Bedouins around schooltime. With the Lord's guidance, the children made more progress with homeschool than they ever would have otherwise.

One of my most difficult times was telling our oldest son, John, goodbye because it was necessary for him to attend college in the States. He had tried to attend Kuwait University of Kuwait, but this too didn't work out because of the language problems.

JIM AND SHIRLEY CARROLL

Altogether, it had already been a tough two years, and now Jimmy was trapped in Kuwait.

But as I sat in our kitchen in Augusta worrying about Jimmy, I remembered all the good times in Kuwait. The best times were our visits with the Bedouins. Their families were huge and multigenerational. Our children played for hours with their children, and language was never a barrier. We sat together as women, drank tea, and sometimes prepared food or ate together. The women took us further into the desert by ourselves, and our children rode the camels and learned the behavior of the animals of the desert, including the snakes. Sometimes the children were left to play in the Bedouin neighborhood while I drove the women to the *souq* to shop. Um Salem was in charge, and she often insisted on bargaining for pieces of gold jewelry for me. They named me Sheika.

The high point of our friendship came when the female children and I were invited to be part of a wedding for one of the younger women. They took me shopping and told me what to buy for each of our girls. Then they brought me to their dressmaker where a dress was especially made for me. Our hands were painted with the traditional henna. We danced at the female portion of the wedding. It was an honor to be called their friend. These were memories I will always hold dear.

FAITH IN CRISIS

Visiting with the Bedouin women

Even the Bedouin camels became our friends

JIM AND SHIRLEY CARROLL

Tim, Lydia, Ruth, Rebecca, and Matthew in a Bedouin home

Left to right: Rebecca, Matthew, Peter holding
Lydia, Rania, and Timothy

FAITH IN CRISIS

Jim holding Lydia

###

A week after I heard about the invasion, I began to unpack our clothes and the schoolbooks we had planned to take back with us. One of the children asked, "Mom, why are you unpacking?"

I replied, "You need to wear the clothes. And we need the school books, so we're unpacking everything."

The best thing for the children and me was to start school and be busy. Our plan was to do homeschool in Kuwait, and we would do the same in Augusta.

The children and I prayed for Papa to come home. "Please, help our dad to be safe in Kuwait. Please, don't let him get captured." We prayed for everything to be all right among our friends in Kuwait and especially for Rania and our Bedouin friends. How would God handle all this?

I remembered the sadness I had experienced for the many years I was unable to get pregnant and then there I sat with six little children and one more in college. God had blessed us as a family, and He was able to do it again any way he chose. We just didn't know how yet.

As the children and I sat at the table for morning devotions I said, "I don't think we'll be going back to Kuwait in two weeks." I told them about what I heard on CNN, and we all listened to the news together. Peter and Ruth understood. Lydia was only three, and Tim and Matt were five. Rebecca was seven, Ruth was ten, and Peter was fourteen. Each one tried to grasp what they were able to absorb from the news and me. "Where's Papa now?" "Where do you think he went when Kuwait was attacked?" "Did he get out with the Bedouins?" "Are we going to hear from him?" "What are we going to do without him?" "When are we going back to Kuwait?"

"I just don't know, but God is always good and He'll provide a time and place for each of us. We went there as missionaries, and God still has a mission for your dad there. He's just where God wants him to be." This was not something I said just to make the children feel better. In my heart, I believed this.

August 8 and the following days

It soon hit me we didn't have a source of income. What could we do? Could I get to our stocks or our bank accounts?

John, a local attorney, and Diane from church came over to help me look at our finances. John said, "We have to establish a budget to make your money stretch as far as it can." It was quite simple: I had no money, and therefore there was no budget. We didn't get that last check from Jimmy, and all I had was some cash I had planned to use on the trip back to Kuwait for food and tips, etc. And the Kuwaiti money I had was no longer usable. Kuwait was no longer a country.

I tried to sell some of our stock, but the broker said I couldn't since it was in both our names. The accountant gently informed I

FAITH IN CRISIS

could sell if I had Jimmy's death certificate. I thought about selling our house, although I was very thankful for a place to live. I soon realized I could sell nothing, nor could I get any money because everything was in our name jointly. The bank couldn't lend me money since I had no job, no collateral I owned on my own, no income and seven children.

John gave me advice I didn't want to hear: "Call the mortgage company, Georgia power, and the Augusta utilities and ask that your bill be waived until you can pay it. Nothing needs to be proved since all the details of what's happening are in the *Augusta Chronicle*." Jimmy's picture had been all over the local paper with the story of the Iraqi invasion.

It occurred to me I could deliver newspapers. I would just pile all the children into the car and go from house to house. However, I was not allowed to do this because they said I couldn't take the children with me. There were too many young ones to stay by themselves.

For a while I tried to sell Avon products. I soon discovered I couldn't sell anybody anything. The only people who bought from me were those who felt sorry for me.

Diane called me every day and prayed with me about the situation. She was honest and tried to help. "You need to tell the children that Jimmy may never come home again."

But I couldn't see this as part of our future. I believed God had a plan for us and that it included us all being a family together again. "I can't tell the children Jimmy's not coming home. I'll work up to any reality in the future, but right now I can only tell the children what I really believe." I believed Jimmy was coming home or that we would return to Kuwait. I knew in my heart he was okay, but no one outside the family believed me. And the children? They just believed he'd be okay.

We were soon running out of food to feed all the little mouths. Concern over Jimmy's situation had not curbed their appetites.

JIM AND SHIRLEY CARROLL

The neighbors began to come to our rescue. I got hundreds of dollars from various neighbors in our little Mayo subdivision. Accepting the money really generated a very difficult time for me, because I never thought I would have to take money from anyone for anything. I looked into food stamps, and learned I was not eligible because we owned our own home. Neighbors began to bring in full grocery bags of food. The children were delighted to see frosted flakes and peanut butter and various items, which I usually did not bring home from the grocery.

Also I no longer had a vehicle to drive. The missionary loan car that we had been using for the summer was due back at the agency for another homebound missionary. Another missionary friend drove the car up to Pennsylvania to return it for me.

The Watts family from our church donated a car to the church for us to use. The church elders and various members came back frequently to visit. They brought meals and money the church had collected. We were never hungry, and the Lord provided. The people in our church prayed for us continually. Every Sunday we sat there in church as Pastor Oliver prayed for us.

One elder visited and was shocked to see several of the kids were sleeping on the floor for lack of available beds. When we first left for Kuwait they had been in cribs, and the cribs could no longer hold them. We had not bought furniture for the girls' room when we came back for the summer. There had been no need because we had planned to go right back to Kuwait. The church provided a large brown bunk bed and trundle set that slept three, which was perfect for our three girls.

Our clothes had been left in Kuwait, but our lack of clothes was no problem for God. People gave us clothes we needed, and I had two friends who made beautiful dresses for the girls. The clothes and food I could accept gratefully, but it was tough for me to take the money, especially from people I knew did not have money to give away. That was not a lesson I wanted to learn.

FAITH IN CRISIS

The people from the Medical College of Georgia where Jim had been employed in Augusta before we went to Kuwait gave us money and brought food. Tom Swift, Jim's former boss, set up a fund for us. The fact I had to accept money from people bothered me so much I couldn't even manage to write thank-you notes. I gave this job to our oldest daughter, Ruth, who was ten years old, and she handled that task for me.

The love shown by the people in the community made me aware even more of God's love for us and his protection in every situation. I had a real peace that Jim would come home, although I had no factual knowledge of this.

As part of our day-to-day routine, I tried to keep very busy. No problem. With six children at home and John coming home on weekends, there was no time to feel sorry for myself. We did schoolwork all the time and accomplished a great deal. I saw that our oldest son at home, Peter, needed a male figure and sports activity. Again, trying to not be hindered by my own pride, I went to the "Y" and asked for a soccer scholarship. They were most gracious in giving this to us. Since we all went everywhere together, I had Rebecca, age seven, with me. She blurted out at the "Y," "Mama, can I take gymnastics?" They allowed her, too, to enroll in a class. Was it a coincidence she turned out to have a gift for the sport? Her God-given gift took her from Augusta to Russia later on.

A friend in our church gave piano lessons to Ruth. I tried not to think about what was in the news and focused my attention to what God's word had said to me. I tried also not to think about Rania and all the people we knew from Kuwait. We were in Augusta now and the Lord had blessed us tremendously by allowing us to stay in our house and provide for all of our needs. We focused upon our gratitude to Him for the many blessings He had given us. I also had an assurance that He was taking care of Jim wherever he was.

JIM AND SHIRLEY CARROLL

The Lord had become a constant companion, because I knew there was so little control I had over the situation and so little I could do. The children and I never entertained any possibility Jim would not return. We talked about going back to Kuwait, seeing Rania and our friends, and getting back our possessions. We had no hatred or bad feelings toward Saddam Hussein or any other Iraqis. The Lord protected us from these emotions and allowed us to know only that everything was part of His plan. Life became a supernatural realization of the peace of the Lord and His presence in our lives.

Chapter 3

Jim on the Run

I was now a self-made fugitive from the Iraqi regime, which had installed itself as the new, legitimate government of Kuwait. I didn't know if the Iraqis wanted me or not, but I did not intend to offer myself up.

August 7–9

The Iraqis had little interest in Third World nationals, but, as I would learn, my US and Brit friends were bigger prizes.

Even from the beginning I wondered if the Iraqis were interested in Americans. Then the news came the Iraqis had taken Edward, a British acquaintance of mine from the National Evangelical Church of Kuwait (NECK) community. The phones continued to work, and a phone call from Ella in the community alerted me to the problem.

"They've taken Edward. He and his wife, Norma, were detained after they approached a checkpoint. The Iraqi soldiers were about to let them pass, and then something happened. They took the car, but let Norma go." Ella continued her alarm, "They forced Edward to go with them. They told her they were going to take him to the police station, and no one knows what happened after that. Norma hasn't seen or heard from him for two days. She's scared to death for him."

I knew Edward as a fellow member of the NECK, the large church for Westerners and Third World Christians down by the Gulf. I questioned the caller. "What happened at the stop? There must be more to it."

She knew only minimal details. Edward reportedly got aggressive and was taken away by the Iraqis. I knew Edward to some degree, enough to know he could be abrasive and difficult to deal with if he was riled. Surely this was the reason he was taken. I consoled myself that the event did not yet constitute a pattern.

I had avoided driving, and now was not the time to take it up again. I had no place to go anyway, and I could get food from the local cooperative market several blocks away

The news of Edward's capture spread fast over the Western expatriate community. We still didn't know the Iraqis' plan for certain toward Westerners, and maybe the Iraqis didn't either. Their strategy wasn't clear to us, but the possible risk increased by the day.

But soon we knew of more abductions of Americans and Brits, and the pattern of these captures took shape either on the street from their vehicles or taken from their homes. Rumors spread fast, and taking into account that there were inherent wartime exaggerations, if at least half were true, I was in trouble. It was real—the next stage of their consolidating the invasion. We were high-worth catches.

Saddam had concluded we were of value. I heard it said among the Arabs, "Saddam is too honorable to take civilian hostages.

FAITH IN CRISIS

He would never stoop to that level. He's like Saladin." Saladin was the Muslim warrior of Crusade times who was known for his courage and integrity, greater than Richard the Lionheart. Okay—then why was Edward gone? Why have the others been taken? Saddam's only commonality with the great Saladin was that both were born in Tikrit in northern Iraq.

The Iraqi management of the invasion amazed me. Even though the Iraqis had destroyed the international phone communications, they allowed local calls to be made without interference. Was this neglect by design or just their ineptitude? We never knew why they allowed the open local phone lines. Was the Kuwaiti resistance using the system? Perhaps the Iraqis were listening in, but how could they listen to thousands of calls? Still we were careful what we said on the phone, resorting to minimal use of names and avoidance of stating locations.

The Iraqis announced we would have to get ration cards in order to get food, more evidence they were consolidating control of the city. I walked to the coop three blocks away and stood in line to get the card with the locals who were in the same situation. Should I give them my information, my civil ID card? Maybe they were using the process to collect information on the citizens in the area. Certainly this was the case, but still I needed food. Uncomfortable, I stood in line with Kuwaitis, mostly women, and I was obviously the only Westerner in the group. I spoke to several. "*Salaam-alaikum*," I said, trying to make conversation with those near me, but they were reluctant to respond to me. Did they consider me a risky acquaintance? I signed up, got the card, and walked back to my house.

Was there a way to get out of here? Was it safer to stay or go? I had two cars, but neither was suitable for travel over the desert without benefit of a road, and the highways were studded with checkpoints. Perhaps I could go out over the desert with my Bedouin friends. I phoned their home in Ahmadi but there was no answer, no answer with multiple calls. Maybe I should drive down to their home and check around. But the Iraqis were heavily occupying that area because of the oil wells. The Bedouins probably had enough sense to get out right away anyway.

I ate several meals with Haddad and his family. In their home it was almost normal. After dinner, Haddad brought out the Chivas. Alcohol was illegal in Kuwait, but this was no impediment to any middle or upper class Kuwait resident. I was just too anxious to accept his offer of a drink. The alcohol might make me less able to cope with an emergency, whatever that might be. I was vigilant about everything. Was I followed? Were the Iraqi patrol cars looking for me?

Haddad, a Jordanian with Palestinian roots, probably had no reason to fear the Iraqis. His children were bored not being able to go visit their friends or attend school, and their fear was less than mine.

I was stuck in my big house with its three floors, multiple bedrooms, huge living room and dining room, tiled kitchen and den. How much time could I occupy walking through all the rooms? I never realized how much an invasion limited one's activities. I was trapped in my own home, a self-made hostage. Haddad fed me in his home from time to time, but mostly I was stuck because of my fear of capture. What a crazy way to think.

Then, finally, the concerns of my being taken hostage amassed, and I could think of little else. What if there was a knock on the door in the middle of the night? How would I make my escape? I went up to the third floor, little used by us as a family. The house was old, and the two top floor bedrooms were dirty with plaster falling from the deteriorating walls and ceilings, and the dust, which seeped into every house in Kuwait, had not been disturbed. We hadn't bothered to keep these rooms orderly, and now they were really a mess. In both bedrooms and in the hall there were windows, which opened out onto the roof.

FAITH IN CRISIS

Here was the plan: if the house was invaded, I would run up the stairs, climb out the window onto the roof, close the window behind me, and stay put behind our water tank. Sure, that's gonna work. The best plan I could come up with was to hide behind the water tank on a roof where the temperature exceeded 130 during the day.

Why were we in Kuwait anyway? Recriminations abounded. I left a good job in the States. The Kuwaitis probably thought we came for the money. Wrong. We had more money and a bigger salary in the States, and we were dipping into our savings each year to stay. We had the idea to come to Kuwait to spread the gospel to Muslims in Kuwait. We were "called." Was God responsible for this? Was this His payback for my pride, that we could do some great thing for Him?

As tools to assist us in our missionary task, we had piles and piles of papers and books on Muslim evangelism. The paperwork identified us as missionaries. What if the Iraqis came into the house and went through all our materials? It would be obvious we were there for a purpose other than just a secular job. They would think: *Is he a missionary or a spy or both?* My value as a hostage would double.

I had to get rid of all those materials. I couldn't go ask advice from Haddad, or from our friends, Asif and Suhair, down the street. They weren't supposed to know about our missionary status. What about burning the materials? The kitchen wall and floor was all tile, and the sink was steel. If I could avoid the wooden cabinets, I could keep from setting the kitchen on fire. I brought all the papers into the kitchen and got out the matches. My plan was to set them on fire in the sink so I could extinguish the flame if necessary. The first papers were difficult to ignite, but after I got it going, I realized it was going to be a mess. The particles of charred paper floated about the kitchen. It was raining charred paper. The smoke had nowhere to go, even when I turned on the kitchen fan. After only one set of papers, the clutter was out of control. Bad idea.

I settled on an alternate plan. I waited until dark and after the first round of Iraqi patrols enforcing the curfew had just gone through the neighborhood. The Iraqis were nervous about their patrols, because the rising Kuwaiti resistance saw the night as their best opportunity to shoot a few of the invaders. I didn't want to be mistaken for a combatant.

I gathered up all the materials and passed by our own packed full garbage containers. There was no way I was going to put them in my own garbage. I rounded the corner to the right and walked two blocks. Most houses seemed unoccupied; at least their lights were out. How had they departed? Surely not everyone had been out of Kuwait for the summer heat break. I found a house that looked unoccupied with the garbage container in front. I put the papers into their garbage container and hurried back to our house. Now these poor people were the ones at risk, and I briefly imagined their incredulity when the Iraqi accused them of being missionaries.

But the Iraqis were no better at looking for missionaries than they were at anything else. Looking back on it now, I see how pitiful most were as soldiers. If I had been discovered, it would have been through an accident.

But I perceived the net around me continuing to close. Was it my paranoia or a realistic assessment? Our TV had been stolen earlier in the year when we were all in the US. We had given up on getting it back and purchased a new one. My neighbor across the street, of Iraqi origin, came over to see me. "Jim, I understand from the Iraqis who've taken over the police station that they've recovered your TV. If you just go down to the station, you can reclaim it." Right. No way. Are you kidding?

"Thanks for all you help on this. I'll go right away." I lied. So much for the goodwill of the Iraqi neighbor. Was he really in contact with the Iraqis at the police station? If so, I certainly couldn't trust him.

Then the big threat was delivered. Haddad came over to speak with me. "The Iraqi colonel in charge of the hospital wants to see you. I think you'd better go. He wants you to report to the staff meeting. It's you responsibility. You're the head of the pediatric unit, and you must be there." Haddad had changed his tune, and now he was asking me to go back to the hospital. For the summer staffing of the hospital, I had been named the unit director. Haddad was right in that sense, and it was my responsibility on paper. Was Haddad dutifully relaying the message, or was he now a shill for the Iraqis? He was of Palestinian origin, and they had sided with Iraq. Once again, my paranoia surfaced. But I was unfair. Haddad had always been my friend. I had sunk to mistrust of a colleague for no reason.

But here was an invitation to be taken hostage. I was done staying in my house. They knew my address, and they would come for me soon.

August 10–13

I had to get out of my house permanently. There was no way I could sleep knowing the knock on the door could come any time. I phoned Suhair and Asif who lived on our block. They were professors who taught in the undergraduate program at Kuwait University. Shirley had met Suhair on the plane during her first trip to Kuwait, and soon after our arrival we discovered we were neighbors. Our two families had spent time together on weekends for barbecues, and our children played together. Their postgraduate degrees were from the US, and their English was excellent. Our communication was unimpeded by our own inadequacy in Arabic.

JIM AND SHIRLEY CARROLL

They knew by this time Western hostages were being taken, and still Suhair agreed to take me in. She was a well-spoken, uncovered woman with glasses and a precise manner. I couldn't believe how gracious she was. "You're welcome to stay with us. You're not safe there in the house by yourself. Everyone knows the Iraqis are looking for you and all the other US citizens and Brits."

Asif was out of the country in Saudi Arabia at the time of the invasion and couldn't get back into the country. Since I couldn't stay with Suhair without a male family member in the house, she had to phone her brother, Ali, and ask him to stay with us, too. We expect fellow Christians to be gracious in times of need. Suhair was a Muslim, mostly secular, but still a Muslim. Even so, she extended hospitality to me at the risk of herself and her children, not to mention the inconvenience. I was a guest that ate every meal, and I slept in the utility room alongside the washer and dryer.

There I was with Suhair's family for days and nothing to do but listen to the BBC ("THIS is the BBC" as they said in those days, and everyone listened) and watch the Kuwaiti TV stations, which had been taken over by the Iraqis. Even after all these years, I recall Suhair did her best to make me feel comfortable.

We all laughed at the Iraqi on TV who had been nominally placed in charge of the new government. He donned the white Kuwaiti *dishdasha*, *gutra* and *aqal*, but he wore the headgear without the usual Kuwaiti jaunty angle, and the poor guy looked uncomfortable in what was, for him, a costume. He was clearly a fake. His job on TV was to pretend he was the rightful representative of the Kuwaiti people.

But the fake Kuwaiti was part of the Iraqi plan. The ongoing theme the Iraqis tried to establish was that Kuwait was taken over because the Kuwaiti people had rebelled against the emir and had demanded the Iraqis come in, a coup requested by the population. The Iraqi army brought down a busload of Iraqi civilians and paraded them around as Kuwaitis chanting slogans in favor of the

FAITH IN CRISIS

Iraqi invasion and take over. Iraqi film crews were on hand, but the Iraqis just couldn't manage to look like Kuwaitis. While the Kuwaiti resistance fought on and civilians were being assaulted, the Iraqis pretended to be welcome invaders. Once again it was all the rumors typical of war, the assaults on civilians, the looting— all the stories, and we had no way to separate lie from truth.

An American family who attended the NECK with our family phoned and asked me to come and stay with them. How had they known where I was? The husband worked in Kuwait for a large US company. "We know you're by yourself without your family; you could come over and stay with us."

I decided I was safer with Kuwaitis than with Americans, so I elected to stay with Suhair. Two days later I learned later they had been able to escape Kuwait over the desert. His company had been able to deliver the necessary bribes to get them out. I had not figured out their real reason for calling me. Evidently they didn't want to reveal the plan over the phone line that might be monitored. Another bad mistake on my part, and I tried to put the regret behind me.

The days at Suhair's were strange and sometimes uncomfortable, and it must have been odd for her, too. I wasn't supposed to be there. A man does not stay in an Arab woman's home, especially when her husband was absent.

Bombs broke the boredom. There were still explosions periodically throughout the city. Who knows what the Iraqis were going after, perhaps the home of a resistance fighter, maybe a strategic location, or just a random act to keep the population frightened.

Several of the explosions were near Suhair's house. Those families still in the neighborhood—and there were many, more than I ever thought—came out of their homes and gathered in the street. They had been sequestered from the patrolling Iraqis, but the bombing brought them out in fear. The women and children were then taken into the basement of one of the few houses that actually had a basement. Men weren't allowed to go into the refuge with the women.

I recall the feeling I had with the explosions: it was exhilaration. The explosion provoked the thought something was going to happen. If there were enough explosions, enough disasters, then a conclusion would come, any conclusion. The waiting day after day for something to happen, something to change, was exhausting.

Then a new event intervened. Why then with all the explosions and checkpoints were we going to lunch with Suhair's family? I was alarmed at the invitation. For them to think it was safe was a puzzle to me. Perhaps they understood the invasion better than I did. We—Suhair, Ali, her brother, her three children, and me—all piled into the family car for the drive down Fahaheel Expressway to Rumathiya. I had to go for the sake of their offered hospitality, but what if we were stopped at a checkpoint? They were probably okay, but what about me as an American and no passport? I would be taken, I was sure. I scrunched into the backseat with her kids. I just wasn't small enough.

The lunch was like every other lunch with a Kuwaiti family. There was no evidence of the invasion. It was hardly mentioned. The house was neat, and the servants were still present and had done their jobs. I had not known Suhair was from such a well-off family. And where did they get all the food, the chicken, the lamb, the fresh vegetables? The usual meal in an Arab home provided more than anyone could finish, and this meal was no exception. To my relief we made it back to Suhair's without being stopped by the Iraqis.

More journal excerpts from the day to Shirley: *I pray you and the kids are well and emotionally strong.... The waiting is nerve-wracking ... I pray God will use me here with Suhair ... they are being very kind to me.... I don't see any break in this ... I'm afraid I'm going to be here a long time. The Iraqis have officially taken over the hospital and I can't*

FAITH IN CRISIS

return there.... Suhair's mother reminds me a lot of your grandmother except she is a faithful Muslim, not a Christian.... She prays regularly and reads the Quran several hours a day. They say she really does this every day. She is calm and confident in the face of all this. This makes me think there is considerable power in "faith" itself. Maybe the trap is there. We aren't saved by "faith" alone. It must be directed to an object. I don't know who the object of her faith is. And how does this all fit in with Abraham, who believed before Jesus came, before God personally intervened in history? I find it hard to concentrate on the profound when all the other worries intrude, but the matter is still on my mind constantly, in one form or another.

The next sign of deterioration came with the announcement all Westerners were to report to hotels in the city. The Iraqis announced they would "assist" with their departure, but departure to where? US citizens were to report to the International Hotel down by the Gulf. This was a no-brainer. Saddam and his bunch were concocting stories to get Americans and Brits to give themselves up. I heard a few Brits reported to their assigned hotel and were taken prisoner. No Americans cooperated.

I am just furious with myself for not being more aggressive about getting out.... I know there are a few who've made it out ... I sat here like a fool.... I should have headed down to Ahmadi the first thing that night to get out with our Bedouin friends, but that was when the invasion was just beginning.... I pray your life and the children may be a witness there in Augusta.... I know God's plan is best ... forgive me for getting myself into this ... I am burning for you in a way that is the most miserable experience I've ever had.

August 14

I tried various ways to organize or just consider an escape. Then at 11:30 in the evening, I received a call from a Syrian friend. "Professor, the border is open. You can join me and my wife and child." Once again they were generous beyond my conceiving. They must have known I was a risk for them. I would be the only American in a large group of Syrians. I leaped at the chance. Then over the next hour, my anxiety rose again. I prayed to be led by the Spirit. I knew the risks were high, and I had no passport.

No, the risks were too great. I was to be the only American attempting to escape the country and if we were stopped, I would be taken prisoner or killed—I decided not to go. A few hours later, my friend called and said they had been sent back by the Iraqis. The border was not open, and the Iraqis were all over the desert. The days of running for it were over, but I still I dreamed of the dramatic, heroic escape.

I had no way to contact Shirley. What must she think? *I pray you don't think I've been killed. May we see each other soon.*

August 15

Why did I come to Kuwait in the first place? Journaling again. *Pride that I would do some great thing on my own.... I'm sure if you asked anyone in our church about me, they would say I was a humble man ... but my pride is so strong I don't even need to demonstrate it.... If any man has been more blessed than me, I never knew him or knew of him.*

August 16

The thought recurred to me that we're sliding to some kind of conclusion. But of course, there was no conclusion. I couldn't believe how God cut off this part of the world with its marvelous people. They had no chance so it seemed at that point.

Suhair and her family were surely sick of me by this time, but they showed no indications of their impatience. They were amazing. I ate more than any of them, and Suhair no longer had the luxury of her maid.

FAITH IN CRISIS

I tried, but they weren't interested in the Gospel. My comments to elicit conversation were passed over. "Why would God do this? What's the source of your mother's faith?" Nothing brought a response, and they moved the conversation on to nonspiritual topics.

I remembered my past discussions with Asif. He was a thin, good-looking man with a black moustache, an Arab intellectual. Looking back now, I think he fit the description of the Sufi. Everything for Asif devolved to the psychospiritual realm. All our talks, when there was time, ended up in a real or unreal category. Always there was some underlying, deeper meaning that we had not been able to plumb. The Sufi branch of Islam sought the meaning under the meaning, and Asif was the intellectual prototype of the Sufi.

He had been to the US for his graduate degree and attended a Pentecostal church. Their emphasis on the work of the Spirit had drawn him in. There was a time there he considered himself a Christian. But he continued in frustration about faith. He kept going back to Matthew 7:7, "Ask, and it will be given to you; seek and you will find; knock, and it will be opened to you."

He had asked for many things, and failed to receive. He questioned me. "Is my faith defective or is the object of my faith inadequate?" He was an inveterate philosopher, and he wanted an answer—particularly an answer that pleased him.

I had responded, "But are you asking for God's best?" Asif saw his request as a test for God, and he thought God had failed him.

Now here I was asking to get out of my predicament. It was my faith in question.

The stories of violence began to circulate around the community with increasing speed. The Iraqis were unpredictable. They killed or stole, some simply trying to get enough food to survive the ordeal Saddam has imposed on them. The Kuwaiti resistance continued to hassle the Iraqis. After a resistance success, the Iraqis would retaliate and escalate the cruelties.

So many poor workers from the Third World had come to Kuwait for something better, and now this. A story circulated of a Kuwaiti employer asking her Sri Lankan maid if she wanted to go back to her country if her countrymen were evacuated from the invasion. She said, "No, Madame, I not go back. Better I die here."

August 17

By this time I'm sure Suhair and her brother, Ali, wanted me out. I had long overstayed the rules for an Arab guest. Three days is the accepted limit for the desert Bedouin. They had been more than generous, and they were beginning to distance themselves from me. I'm sure they were becoming concerned I was a risk to them and the children.

An imposed solution to my sojourn was provided. We already knew Iraqis were shooting Kuwaitis if they provided any sort of resistance. Then an announcement came over local TV and radio. Any Kuwaitis who harbored British or US citizens were to be killed.

My stay with Suhair was done. I had avoided sheltering in the embassy because I was afraid of being cornered there. But I couldn't delay the decision any longer, waiting until Suhair asked me to leave. I heard there were Americans taking refuge in the US embassy, so I phoned the embassy to see if I could come there. Since I was a doctor, they were happy to have me on board. Little did they know I was an academic pediatric neurologist and therefore of little use in a disaster.

I decided to drive our Chevy station wagon, the more dependable of our two vehicles, to the embassy. I went back to our house down the block from Suhair's and made strategic choices of what to take—old family pictures, emotionally important knickknacks, and the few clothes I might need. I should have taken my winter coat, but with temperatures over 100 it didn't seem necessary. I put on my white doctor coat, draped my stethoscope around my neck, and fired up the old Chevy.

The trip to the embassy had to pass through the city. I tried to plan it out to avoid checkpoints, but I guessed wrong. The Iraqi soldiers were stationed at the corner of Istiqlal Expressway and First Ring Road, and they were stopping cars as they proceeded. I pulled up as high in the seat as I could make myself, made sure my stethoscope and white doctor coat were visible, tried to look confident and superior like a doctor should look, pulled slowly up to the checkpoint, rolled down my window partway, nodded, waved, and continued slowly around the soldiers and the checkpoint. They waved back politely. Nobody stops a doctor on his way to work. They might need my services.

The Iraqis who had been left to guard the city were poor soldiers. I wondered if they would follow orders if a battle ensued. Already they were looking thin and tired. Their equipment looked like army surplus, and their vehicles often just stopped running in the Kuwait summer boil, their engines steaming or smoking.

The rest of the four-mile journey from our house to the embassy was unimpeded, and I soon reached the area around Gulf Road and the Kuwait Towers in the center of Kuwait City. But I didn't know how to enter the embassy, which was on a large corner lot on Gulf road with the sea on the other side of the road. A white concrete wall about ten feet high, several feet thick surrounded the compound, topped with razor wire. The International Hotel was across the side street towering over the embassy with many rooms and balconies looking down on the compound. There was no way for me to remain invisible.

I hated the excessive exposure in the middle of the city, but there was no alternative. I parked the car on the side street between the hotel and the embassy, walked up to the reception

JIM AND SHIRLEY CARROLL

gate, and told the attendant who I was and why I was there. He said, "Drive around to the entry gate in back." When I pulled up, the metal gate went up on its rollers. I parked the car in a row of other vehicles, presumably belonging to others who were in the same predicament.

Chapter 4

The Embassy: August 18-24

The embassy looked nothing like my past visits, which had been sedate and predictable receptions at holiday parties with proper decorations and lights hung around the perimeter on the walls. On this visit there was a big, bustling, and disorganized group of individuals, families, and young children. There were a number of individual men like me who had bumbled into the embassy because there was no other easy sanctuary. At first there were so many people I couldn't tell who was a diplomat and who wasn't. Three laughing blond little girls brushed past me as I tried to introduce myself.

Multiple buildings were spread over the five-acre grounds, all painted white or cream to fit in with the desert architecture: the three-story Marine barracks, the chancery, an embassy receiving area for visa applications, the ambassador's residence, the medical infirmary, the kitchen building behind the pool for outside events,

JIM AND SHIRLEY CARROLL

a shower area beside the kitchen and pool, a building with lots of stored items, including canned food, various tools, and multiple freezers, a large room underground, an all-purpose building on one side of the pool, tennis and volley courts, all on a grassy green tract with a flower garden and date palm trees. There was enough space for all, not luxurious but remarkable in God's provision. Families were scattered all over the compound in attempts to find housing for them.

The new joiners of the big embassy family had formerly lived outside in the city, many expats like myself, and families of diplomats. The Marines who were living in the embassy barracks were also on the grounds. The embassy had taken on all comers. I later gathered this was not the usual practice in countries under siege.

"So you're the doctor. We're really happy you're here. We'll find you a place to sleep and show you the medical office." Just that single statement from the embassy nurse made me feel at home for a moment. The doctor's office, formerly the nurse's desk, was furnished with some basic equipment, an examining table, and old-style EKG machine, a few medications stacked in the corner, and even some vaccines in the refrigerator.

Ambassador Howell had a job I'm sure he never thought he'd have—playing innkeeper to well over a hundred adults and children. By the time of my arrival, there were about 170 souls on the compound. We were in wartime mode, most of us unaccustomed to such turmoil and danger. The plan of the day was getting the large group settled with beds, mattresses, space, and food procurement.

Sleeping quarters were assigned and for a while I bedded down on a mattress on the floor of the living room in the residence. The embassy air conditioner made sleeping conditions pleasant. Each evening I carried a mattress in and placed it on the marble floor near the piano next to the sliding door opening on to the garden.

FAITH IN CRISIS

In the morning I removed the mattress. I had to go to bed late and get up early in order to avoid disturbing the other people living in the residence. No problem—I was too anxious to sleep anyway.

The meals were arranged in glorious fashion. The embassy staff had wisely acquired large food stores as they anticipated it might come to such a state. I was thankful for the food, but I wondered: if they suspected the Iraqis would invade, why hadn't they told us to get out of Kuwait? But those decisions weren't made easily or quickly accomplished, and now it was too late.

A local supermarket was trying to get rid of its stores and make a profit before the Iraqis got around to stealing their food, and the embassy was a happy partner in this endeavor. The entry of the market underground warehouse was made to appear abandoned and was thereby concealed from the Iraqis and referred to as "Aladdin's Cave." For the several early days we ate like kings— with turkey, roast beef—more than I would have had on a typical day at home. I was eating free at the expense of the US government. The embassy kitchen bustled with activity providing for the nervous mob of adults and normally rambunctious children. How could the embassy staff get a handle on all this activity, all the people, and the uncertainty of "How long"? I had to admit the embassy organization was encouragingly impressive, and I felt safe for the moment.

But my feelings were confused. On one hand I was happy to be with other Americans in the same predicament, but I had surrendered some of my freedom by coming into the embassy, and now I worried how it all would be concluded. I didn't know whether to feel better or worse.

I took up the role as "Doc," which was to be my code name. Why did I need a code name? Several of us were given walkie-talkies with which we could communicate with other inmates. Why was I suddenly important enough to have a walkie-talkie? Were we in such a sad state already that I was a critical player?

JIM AND SHIRLEY CARROLL

It was obvious the Iraqis were monitoring our bandwidth. We could hear them at times on the walkie-talkie. The other embassy occupants who stayed there throughout the siege were also given monikers for radio use. I'm still not sure why. I think the embassy staff dreamed it up for our entertainment. And I suppose there was some element of safety tacked on. If we took part in something the Iraqis didn't like, perhaps we could hide behind the little trick. And if we were on calls to others in the community, it might be better we weren't identified. My codename "Doc" was pretty transparent, however. The fact we had code names seemed to confuse the Iraqis and apparently made them think we were more important than we were, and that we had some plan we were executing.

Most of the medical complaints were minor—colds, headaches, and rashes. We had a decent assortment of drugs in the infirmary, and as a pediatric neurologist I dealt with problems to which I was unaccustomed. But there were general medical books, and I could look up simple diagnoses and treatments. An EKG machine was in the infirmary, and its presence was intimidating to me. I had not interpreted adult EKGs since medical school twenty years before. But there was a handbook showing how to put on the leads on and several examples of abnormal EKG interpretation. I could get by and probably identify a heart attack. I didn't bring up my concerns. No point in making the others even more frightened. I was the only doctor option available, and the one nurse was anxious to share responsibility.

One incident set the tone for what was to come: *know nothing and suspect everything*. Over my radio came the request. "Doc, you need to come to the infirmary." Several of the staff came to hurry me to the medical building to see a new patient. It turned out he was not a resident of the compound. The tall, skinny guy looked terrible. He was out of breath, trembling, red-faced, and sweating

FAITH IN CRISIS

profusely, no surprise since it was 120 degrees. I shook his hand and introduced myself.

"Hi, my name is Jim Carroll."

He returned with a short "Hello" but avoided giving his name. After a time I concluded he must have some type of official status or else the staff wouldn't be so interested in him. He didn't have on a uniform. Maybe he was CIA, but I never knew for sure.

And he was distressed. The medical history is critical for diagnosis, and I asked, "Tell me what happened to you. Does anything hurt?" My attempts to solicit information fell flat. All I could get was that he had run to the embassy from Jahra to the west, a distance of more than five miles in the blazing sun. I gathered he had come to report some type of Iraqi activity in the area, and all I could tell for sure was that he was really upset about it. Clearly I was not the person he was supposed to report to. If this guy, supposedly a pro, was so disturbed, maybe I should be worried, too.

I sat him down and asked the nurse, "Please get him some bottles of water." As he was pounding down the fluids, I took his blood pressure. It was 200/120, way high.

"Does he need to go to the hospital?"

I replied, "Are you sure you want him to go to the hospital?" The guy shook his head vigorously. It was too dangerous for him to report to the Iraqi-controlled hospital system unless there was no other choice. I thought he was just overheated, dehydrated, anxious, and scared.

After thirty minutes he regained his composure, and he was gone with one word—"Thanks." I never saw him again. If we had to stay in the embassy, how and why did people like him come and go?

So many rumors. The appearance and disappearance of the tall, thin man who was so upset about what he had observed preyed on me. Worries and fears built on themselves. If even half were true, then something new and awful might happen any time. I prayed not to be taken prisoner to Baghdad. That was my greatest fear. It had been so since day one, and the fear grew.

The new pastor for the church, Maurice Graham, was there. He and his wife, Laurie, and two boys, had just arrived in Kuwait to work for the NECK. Talk about bad timing. Maurice's primary background was in counseling, and he jumped into this role with no shortage of clients. Several women housed at the hotel across the street had been assaulted as they arrived at the airport, and he was assigned to them for the first few days. Everyone involved had been careful not to utter many details.

Maurice was a thin guy with glasses, high-pitched voice, and an intense approach. He had even less hair than I did. I'm not sure why he singled me out. I think he was concerned about my emotional condition, and I was grateful to him for it. Maybe he thought I was high risk. Or more likely he just saw it his role to care for others. He was a good guy. We briefly exchanged our Christian testimonies.

"Let's put together a Bible study." I'm not sure which of us suggested the gathering. We began Bible studies and soon several were attending.

August 19

I learned about something called "war insurance." Were they kidding? Who would have thought such a thing existed? I guess I should have bought some. I thought I was so wise about all the financial arrangements, but I suppose I neglected this alternative. Or maybe the guy who brought it up was just putting me on.

The Iraqis were firmly entrenched. In contrast to the area around our house in the Jabriya section of the city, they were

FAITH IN CRISIS

everywhere along the coast and Gulf Road. I didn't see how the blockade put in place by the US would work. What would be "blockaded"? The Iraqis had everything they needed because they were taking it from the Kuwaitis. The system set up by the Iraqis seemed self-sufficient. Unless the US attacked, I thought, this could go on for years.

I continued writing in my daily journal. It was an exercise for my spirit and a release of anxiety. *Tonight I asked to talk to Maurice about my feeling of desperation. I just felt I was "losing it." He was very kind. I think I may be able to get to sleep.* I still had not landed on the main question in the back of my mind: why had all this happened? The why was not a political question—it was a personal question, a spiritual inquiry. Why had this happened to me? I took it personally.

The Iraqis set the date for the closing of all embassies—August 24. What did the deadline mean? Did it mean we would be taken to Baghdad? Would there be anything that was still called an embassy with diplomats? Will they kill those who remain? I knew I wasn't going anywhere on my own.

The number on the compound rose to a peak of 200. Although the embassy staff had done a marvelous job procuring food, the length of time the supply would last was maybe a month by my estimate. Estimating the speed of food consumption for such a large group, however, had been neglected in my medical school training.

August 20

Maurice said, "You need to stop depending on yourself and look to the Spirit." Sure, but what was the Spirit's message in this? I hadn't been informed, but perhaps the Spirit's message was not favorable for me. At that point the message was not encouraging.

JIM AND SHIRLEY CARROLL

If we had to go to Baghdad, I didn't know what would happen to the women and children. I was sure there would be rapes. *Shirley, I'm so thankful you're not here.*

God put together a group of believers here on the compound: evangelicals, charismatics, those who say they're Christians, otherwise, all ages. A young Marine named Paul was a believer. There were six Marines on the compound. I didn't know what would happen to them if the Iraqis got hold of them. They were at greater risk than I, except for one thing: as a physician, I might be deemed of some value to the Iraqis. It occurred to me I would be scooped up for that purpose to serve their troops, and suddenly there was something else to worry about.

We observed several unexpected events among the Iraqis who surrounded the compound. The Iraqi troops left many of their positions among Gulf Road, departing from the area where we could watch them from the embassy vantage point. Perhaps they were moving back north. Or maybe it was just a normal occurrence of troop rotation or simply a changing of positions. We looked for any sign of something good. We were intent on every variance we observed. All happenings, simple observances that meant nothing, took on meanings we conjured up.

We all thought Saddam needed some way to save face. If the US or the Kuwait government in exile just gave him an excuse to pull back, then he would have an honorable exit. But we saw no sign of honor in him. Our minds searched for any excuse for hope, a way the situation could be defused.

We learned the Iraqis were putting missile placements in Kuwait. Saddam was not signaling any intention to leave.

I heard from Barbara Bodine, the deputy in charge of mission for the embassy, that it might be possible for me to get a contract as an embassy physician. This would generate a little income for the family, though it wouldn't replace what we had before or approach what was needed. *How are you going to feed the kids?*

August 21

The group of believers was a blessing to me. Another man joined the group today. He was one of my patients in the compound and for me the biggest "pain in the butt" we had there. He seemed to have inordinate medical needs. But my view of him changed. He was just scared like me. I did the devotional that night, Romans 8:31–39, and particularly verse 38, "For I am sure that neither death nor life, neither angels nor rulers, nor things present nor things to come, nor powers, nor height nor depth, nor anything else in all creation, will be able to separate us from the love of God in Christ Jesus our Lord." I wanted to show we were receiving God's best, convincing myself of it as much as the others. I knew we were safe in the Lord in any case, but I was frightened and unsure how His plan would be manifest. My "pain in the butt" patient benefitted from the word just as I did.

August 22

The nonessential diplomatic staff was scheduled for evacuation, leaving the private citizens like me behind. I understood it was important to get families and children out as soon as possible before there was open fighting, but the split in the community was a blow to all the folks like me. We were jealous, no two ways about it. The conversation among us civilians escalated.

"What if all the diplomats decided to ditch us?"

"Who could blame them?"

"We were not their only responsibility, and it might turn into a numbers game."

"Which plan could save the most?"

"We might be the losers in that mathematical analysis."

"No, that's wrong."

"We would definitely be the losers."

JIM AND SHIRLEY CARROLL

We were angry with the diplomats and paranoid about the outcome, but we were afraid to say much. Mainly we were just angry God had placed us in this predicament. We were suspicious about the whole process—some of us leaving and some not. I sent a letter to Shirley via one of the women getting out.

> *Dear Shirley,*
> *I am sending this letter via Mary Bender, a nurse at the embassy compound.... Although we could leave by the convoy, the ambassador recommended we not go.... We would likely be separated from the diplomatic staff and sent to undesirable places in Iraq.... Also, I felt that I've been where God wanted me to be at each point.... I'm so sorry I've failed to get back to you... I was afraid of being captured or killed... please forgive me for not making it out yet... I guess I'm just not daring. I want to stay alive and do what God wants me to do.... I pray for you constantly.... By God's mercy and grace, I will return to you.... I hope the power of attorney will be sufficient for whatever you have to do to secure the use of our finances.... I am comfortable and well-fed—no physical problems.... Keep praying. Wait on the Lord.*

I learned much later that Shirley got the letter. There would be many more letters sent and never received by her until I brought them myself.

###

Several adults who were not permitted to leave had children with them and wanted their kids taken to safety. The ambassador arranged "adoptions" for these children so they could accompany the departing diplomatic staff. The parents were frightened for their children in the midst of war, ambivalent about the separation, and uncertain about the wisdom of the "legal" action. With all the legal hassle we had with our adoptions back in the States, how could it be so simple in the embassy in the midst of an occupation? I was thankful not to have to make that decision. Maurice and Laurie Graham decided to keep their two boys with them in the embassy. They couldn't bear to send them out with others.

Bush was talking tough. We thought he was playing dice with our lives. We weren't the focus of the invasion. We knew it had to be the oil in Kuwait and Saudi Arabia. The capture of Kuwait made any advance into Saudi Arabia that much easier for the Iraqis.

But as for us, we were the center of existence.

Arrangements were in process to get the Marines and diplomat families out of the compound and to safety. Saddam said he would allow the official staff, including their children, to drive to Baghdad and fly back to the West. As nondiplomatic staff, we couldn't go. We wanted out, too, and we had unconcealed ambivalence about their release without us. I was happy they could go but jealous I couldn't. Still, the fact they could leave was an encouragement. I might soon go as well. Among those of us remaining, emotional contradictions were the default state on the compound.

I got up at 2:30 in the morning to see the departure of the privileged evacuees. How could I sleep through the momentous event? And moreover, I wanted to make sure I didn't miss some opportunity to get in the convoy. Rules were still subject to the whims of the Iraqis.

The Iraqi escort showed up and said they could take half of the group. The Iraqis were either confused about what their orders said or they were playing mind games, maybe both. It was "We're going," "No, we're not going" for hours. The ambassador was on top of negotiating with the Iraqi leadership. The Iraqi ambassador was the vehicle for carrying on the discussion, but he was not in charge. He had to confer with Baghdad. We couldn't figure out if the difficulty was part of their plan or just administrative incompetence, or some wartime combination of the two.

Finally they were off after three hours of negotiation, and I went back to bed and tried to sleep. Sleep didn't come; I was too revved up.

About 7:30 in the morning, the staff came to get me out of bed. "Doc, you have to come out to the parking lot. There's been a car accident on the road to Baghdad and someone's been injured." They had turned around after the accident and brought her back to the compound. I got to the car and found it was one of the older women, Odessa Higgins. She was still in the vehicle where she had been placed in after the accident. She was alert but in a lot of pain. They drove the car as near the infirmary as possible, and we moved her gingerly into the infirmary. It was painful for her to be lifted with her injuries, but we had no stretcher.

I examined her in the infirmary. She had no bleeding, obvious chest or abdominal injuries. There were no head injuries. Her main trauma was to her left upper leg, and moving her about had made the pain worse. I was pretty sure she had a broken femur, perhaps near the hip joint. I gave her a shot of Demerol. Doctors rarely give injections, and I had not done so for many years. The injection accomplished little in relieving her pain.

There was nothing we could do for her in the compound. She had to go to the hospital for treatment, probably surgery on the hip. How would we get her there? We loaded her back in the car. Her pain was still poorly controlled, but I was hesitant to give her more Demerol. The Marine officer accompanying her said, "Doc, you need to help me get her to the hospital." We had been told the Iraqis would take us prisoner if we left the compound, and now I was being asked to leave with her. There was no medical reason for me to accompany her but I agreed. Not to do so would impair their confidence in me. This was no time to damage my relationships with the embassy staff.

I couldn't abandon her at that point, and I knew the nearest hospital, Amiri, quite well. I had seen pediatric patients there

FAITH IN CRISIS

many times. Their facilities in the past were more than adequate, and their doctors, if they showed up, could handle the medical aspects. Although Odessa would likely require hip surgery, she wasn't in need of life-saving emergency surgery. She was going to be okay. The underlying concern was whether she and her accompanying husband would be turned into hostages. He was stunned by the course of events and followed as the dutiful spouse. Good for him.

We all got in the car and proceeded down Gulf Road to Amiri Hospital. The Iraqis stopped us at a checkpoint. I had no papers, and I was afraid they were going to take me, but we were waved on after the Indian driver was checked. We pulled up to the Amiri casualty department (the emergency room in Arab countries is called the Casualty Department), and we took her inside with a wheelchair. The doctors on duty were busy with other emergencies, and the emergency area was a mess. The formerly clean and sparkling Amiri had been looted and left filthy. Since Odessa was not shedding blood, we had trouble getting her seen, but we finally succeeded in getting her to someone's attention.

The Marine accompanying me was in a hurry to get back to the convoy proceeding north to Baghdad. "I've got to get back to the road before they get too far ahead. I'm supposed to be with my men and the diplomats."

There was no point in either of us remaining with Odessa. I was afraid to stay at the hospital by myself and away from the compound. "I'm going back with you." I wondered if he had planned to leave me there at the hospital. We made our way safely back to the compound where they let me off and proceeded on to Baghdad.

During the ride to Amiri and back, I realized again how bad things were in the city. The Iraqi soldiers were a ragtag, worn-out bunch. Old men and beardless boys were dressed up like soldiers. They were camped in pitiful bivouacs. Deserted Iraqi vehicles were all over the place. They hadn't counted on maintaining vehicles in the terrific heat of the Kuwait summer, and they were burning them up without means of repair or adequate oil. In a country full of oil, they had no means to keep their equipment supplied with lubricant. I was not skilled in assessing troop readiness, but I couldn't see how they would fight a modern army.

Rumors flourished. The Indian driver told me the hospitals were running out of supplies. We heard there was a cholera epidemic working its way south from Iraq. I had a few vials of cholera vaccine in the embassy infirmary, but I knew enough about cholera to know that the vaccine was relatively ineffective.

We didn't know what was rumor and what wasn't. I knew from war stories that inaccuracies thrived and were propagated in such circumstances, and now I saw it firsthand.

In the afternoon I got another offer from a couple staying in the embassy to go out through the desert. "We have a CIA friend. He gave us a map of the Iraqi troop placements. We can definitely rely on this info, it's firsthand. We're going out on our motorcycles." Again I decided against it. Good thing I had never ridden a motorcycle, because that was the deciding factor of the moment. The CIA connection sounded enticing, and there was hope their information was accurate.

All sorts of groups were trying to figure out where the Iraqis were in the desert. The theory developed that south over the open desert and into Saudi Arabia was the exit route of choice. The path might have been viable two weeks ago, but now there was no chance—there were just too many Iraqis. Sure they were pretty pitiful, but they were all over the place, like roaches in a sugar mill.

Ian Siller was a twenty-four-year-old young man. He had just finished school and had come to Kuwait as a math teacher

FAITH IN CRISIS

at the American School of Kuwait. He was not a Christian but he was interested in spiritual matters. He was a New Ager, so any discussion, any idea, was fair game. I was amazed how pervasive the New Age movement was among the Westerners trapped here. New Agers envision a holistic, universal concept of divinity, including their own, intimate participation in the system. There is thus a strong emphasis on the spiritual authority of the self.

We had some good theological discussions, and he was somewhat open to the gospel but not in any exclusive sense. "I think there are a lot of ways to get to heaven. Islam has a lot of positives. I have respect for Christians, too." He was a big man, an exercise buff and full of big muscles, maybe a good friend to have under such circumstances.

With Ian I had a different sort of experience in friendship evangelism. There were two small dogs left in the compound, and Ian had taken the responsibility for them. Two departing diplomatic families had left their dogs behind under his care.

The dogs became an issue. Ian said, "I wish I hadn't taken the responsibility. I don't know what to do with them. We can't take food away from the people here to feed dogs."

"If we turn the dogs loose outside the embassy, the Iraqis will eat 'em. We can't feed the Iraqis." The Iraqis had already begun to consume Kuwait's vast camel herd. Even the *dhubs* (large spiny-tailed lizards) in the desert weren't safe.

We had to kill the dogs. The reasoning was clear, or so it seemed in that crazy time. If we gave them to Iraqis, they would probably eat the dogs. They obviously did not have enough to eat, and the dogs would be a treat for them. If we kept them in the compound, they would eat the food the humans needed. If we left the compound and the dogs remained, they would starve.

So we resolved to put them down as humanely as possible. I got some injectable Valium from the infirmary, as much as I thought would be needed. The dogs were about fifteen pounds apiece, and it shouldn't take much Valium to finish them. I converted a dose that would suppress breathing in an adult human to one appropriate for the dogs' weight. I gave the injections in their hindquarters, and we waited about ten minutes. The dogs didn't turn a hair, and I gave another round. Nothing. I tried once more on one of the dogs and still not much. He was a little drunk but still walking around. We might need it more for the humans later on, and I couldn't use any more of the infirmary Valium supply.

But we were now committed to the project. We got a rope and wrapped it around each dog's neck one at a time. Ian was strong and had no trouble holding the dogs down while I choked each animal with the rope. I had no idea it took so long to kill an animal by strangulation, and I was exhausted by the time the second dog died. We took their bodies and buried them in the garden behind the embassy residence. The day was not one of my medical triumphs. I had an odd sense of completion and spiritual defeat at the same time. I was a dog-killing missionary.

###

A day later we learned the Iraqis had lied about releasing everyone for the fly out from Baghdad. The men of the large group who left with the promise of getting out of Iraq were held up in Baghdad. We could only pray they were safe. They kept all adult males, even the teenage boys, prisoners in Baghdad. Only the women and children were allowed to leave the country. So much for trusting the Iraqis—if there ever had been such an idea. This was not in conflict with my line of thinking, because I had long since decided not to trust them.

The number of residents continued to shrink. Many had left for various reasons, some because they thought they would be safer on their own. Not me—I'd been through that exercise, and I was stuck for the duration, whatever that might be.

FAITH IN CRISIS

The next day was August 24, the date the Iraqis set for the closing of the embassies. We didn't know what that meant. If we no longer had diplomatic protection, why couldn't they just come into the embassy and take us away? Without the status of the embassy, we were just like any other American hiding out in an apartment. Even the diplomats might no longer have immunity. We were comforted by the word they had not hurt any Americans, but as the situation became more extreme, who knew? It was one new worry after another. Our minds and conversations ran wild with speculation. And the fragments we got from the community information system the diplomats had in place and from the TV news we received fueled our speculation. We didn't have enough to do to keep us occupied, and worry was the first alternative. One among us commented, "They're going to be in here after us tomorrow. You can bet on it. This is what they've been waiting for. The ambassador won't be the ambassador anymore."

###

August 24 – Shirley

The strange call from the State Department came at 9:00 AM. "Is this Mrs. James Carroll? I'm calling to inform you that Dr. Carroll is in the US embassy in Kuwait."

"Is he all right?"

"The only thing I know is that he's in the embassy…."

"Can I talk to him?

"No, you can't."

"What about messages?"

"There's nothing we can do on that."

"When will I hear something more?"

"We don't know. We'll call if there is any information."

"Wait."

Click.

JIM AND SHIRLEY CARROLL

Thank the Lord—I had finally heard about Jimmy from the State Department. I gathered the children together and told them Papa was being held hostage in the American embassy in Kuwait, and he was safe. We thanked the Lord for this news and again I felt sure everything would be all right.

Chapter 5

Iraq Closes the Embassies

August 24

The Iraqis closed off the embassy compound just as they promised. That was one pledge they kept. There were two main entry or exit points for the embassy compound: the back gate through which I had driven my car a week earlier and the front gate where most visitors had formerly entered. Bullet-resistant glass at each entry point provided a portal through which to see and inspect visitors. But there would be no more visitors. As far as the Iraqis were concerned, we were no longer an embassy, and our legal status under international law was uncertain.

The Iraqis posted guards at these two sites and at additional points around the perimeter of the property, and the rules were clear to us and specifically understood by all. First, no one could enter. Second, while we were technically free to leave, we knew if we did we would then be subject to the will of the Iraqis. We no longer enjoyed our rights as American citizens or residents of Kuwait.

The soldiers set up small, leaning tentlike structures for shelter from the sun around the compound perimeter. As pitiful as the soldiers were, they still carried machine guns. The crack Republican Guard troops with their spiffy uniforms began to disappear and sad-looking conscripts replaced them.

One pair typified the replacements. The younger of the two—I hesitate to say he was man—was thin, no muscles, no beard, pale, and a facial expression betraying dread of his predicament. I suppose he feared us, and maybe he was more frightened than I was. His partner was a middle-aged man, perhaps fifty, overweight, and balding. From his labored gait and movements, my neurological diagnosis was that he had Parkinson's disease. Were they straight off the streets of Baghdad? Such were our guards. Did they have enough training to know when not to shoot?

As a fitting emphasis for the day, we heard the group that left the compound before the shutdown was captured attempting to cross the desert. Barbara Bodine, the deputy in charge of mission (DCM) for the embassy, code name Kestral (a small falcon), delivered the news in front of several of us in the evening by the pool. "Those people who left two days ago we've heard were taken by the Iraqis when they tried to cross the desert. They're probably headed for Baghdad right now."

Barbara was a plain-speaking, serious woman who rarely minced words, and she wanted to make certain we got the message about the fate of the departees. Although the group thought they had good information about Iraqi positions, the reports had been out of date by at least several days. Perhaps Barbara delivered this information to us in order to accentuate our vulnerability if we decided to leave. Much appreciated. We got the point.

We understood the group was transferred to Baghdad to serve as "guests" in the "Human Shield" program. What a great, clean-sounding name, and they could participate in a "program." We assumed they were taken to sites critical to Iraqi defense to be held there hoping their presence would prevent US bombing. If there was ever any doubt the Iraqis were taking Western, civilian hostages, we had long since dispensed with that debate. It was either hide out there in the embassy or take chances on the street. No such risk for me, at least not until we dreamed our dreams of miraculous escapes.

My journal entries to Shirley continued. Would she ever read them? *Pray I'll continue to be led by the Spirit ... I'm praying not be taken to Baghdad.*

What would happen if the Iraqis entered the embassy? I pictured their incursion: tough-looking, muscular young men bearing black Saddam moustaches, carrying AK-47s, and pushing their way in and over the gate. Certainly not the frightened adolescent or the disabled middle-aged man. Since we were in their eyes no longer an embassy, would they use our new loss of status as permission to come into the embassy? Would we be just like every other residence they had entered and sacked? Would there be fighting of some sort?

The utilities were intact for the first day of the closure. We had enough food and water to last months, much longer after so many had left. The food stores in the embassy were vast. We could make it on our own for a very long period. But how long would it be? If I just had a date, I could relax until then.

Now that we were closed off in semi-sovereignty, it was time for us to learn the nature of our little nation state. Ambassador Howell gathered us all for a compound conference and made it clear he wouldn't allow us to fight back. Howell, code name 99 (we would much later come to call him "Nat," for Nathaniel), was a large man with white hair, full beard, and an imposing manner. He had no trouble making it clear he was in charge.

There would be no fighting the Iraqis. We would have to surrender immediately if they entered. Would they take us prisoners peaceably, or would there be violence? The ambassador had wisely secured or destroyed all weapons available on the compound. He probably had his own private stash, but we would never see these.

Howell delivered his no-more-democracy speech in the embassy residence on the afternoon of the twenty-fourth. He was the captain, and about that fact he left little doubt. He made every effort to assure us he would not leave without us. "When we leave, we all leave together." In order to achieve the embassy objectives, everyone would have a job. Howell knew he had to keep us occupied—no idle hands here.

The ambassador anticipated the arrival of a fuel truck from one of his still-functioning contacts in the city the day of the forced embassy closure. The gasoline would power the available generators and replace electricity if it was turned off. But the time of the closure was altered to a time earlier in the day, a surprise to the ambassador, and the Iraqis turned the fuel truck away at the back gate. The sight and sound of the big diesel truck pulling up to the gate was inspiring, but its backing up and departure was a blow. The ambassador's negotiations with the Iraqi commander couldn't undo the refusal.

The main concern had been securing fuel for long-term communication purposes, and now that ability was at greater risk. Aside from food and water, communication with the State Department remained the enduring need. We could survive without electricity for lights and air conditioning. The main purpose for the additional fuel was to make certain the embassy could continue to communicate with the State Department for however long our forced encampment lasted. If an Iraqi incursion occurred, we had to maintain sufficient communication to notify

FAITH IN CRISIS

the US. Now another limit was imposed on our existence in the compound. The Iraqis meant business.

###

About seventy of us remained in the compound in these early days. The departure of the diplomat families and Marines had removed a large number of mouths to be fed, but there were still many others—families with children who had sought refuge, men who had obvious medical illnesses and had no business in such a dilemma, the eight remaining diplomats, and the rest of us.

The permanent group on the compound began to take shape. The Raytheon engineers who had been responsible for teaching the Kuwaitis how to operate their newly acquired Improved Hawk missile batteries were sequestered in the embassy, for their protection but mainly to make certain their abilities didn't fall into the hands of the Iraqis. One of these, my friend Benny, code name "Chicken," joined us for Bible studies. Benny was about my height, 5'9", brown hair, younger than me, already missing his Filipina wife. Felipe was older, a former military vet, seemingly knowledgeable about military strategy, and a great source of conversation in our endless discussions about the course the coming battle would take. Two others of the Raytheon group decided to make it on their own and left the embassy.

Benny and Felipe had been in Kuwait instructing the Kuwaiti military about the operation of their new missile batteries. If Benny and Felipe fell into the hands of the Iraqis, they might be forced to share their information about the Hawks. The Iraqis had captured the batteries before they could be fired or destroyed. The embassy staff had taken the passports of Benny and Felipe to make sure they wouldn't be identified if they were taken. My initial chief affinity with them was my lack of a passport, the one I had turned in just before the invasion for our residency update. Thus, the three of us were together in our predicament without passports.

Ron Webster, code name "Longhorn," and Jack Rinehart, had multiple practical skills that would turn out to be critical to the continuing operation of the embassy. If it was broken, they could probably fix it.

Two of the others were knowledgeable about weapons of various types. They claimed to be sales agents to countries in need of arms. I learned more than I wanted to know about modern weapons packages. There were numerous copies of *Jane's Weapon Systems* scattered around the embassy, and we looked up the armaments that surrounded us. Why did an embassy need this reading material? But the magazines were a great source for identifying the various weapons that passed by or set up around the embassy.

###

Sitting in the newly closed embassy, I kept thinking of the Bible passages that dealt with asking for one's desires. Asif, Suhair's husband, was hung up on that, and now I was, too. I recalled the long weekend afternoons with his haranguing over this one point, his major point of argument against Christianity. If God didn't supply what Asif requested from God, even though he had promised to do so, what kind of God was He? It was an endless discussion, and now I shared Asif's thoughts. I focused on Romans 8:28, "And we know that for those who love God all things work together for good, for those who are called according to his purpose." The difference was the last phrase of Romans 8:28. We were called for "his purpose," not mine. I got that part of the text and believed the whole thing, but I still didn't know why all this was happening to me. For this single issue, Romans 8:28, I was the center of the universe.

And yet there I was asking Him to get me out. We prayed for some good news, but the situation only escalated. If war began, there was a good possibility I wouldn't make it out. There were just too many Iraqis. Why should the US bother with the few remaining individuals in the embassy when the lives of thousands of invading US troops were at stake? Wouldn't they take priority? They couldn't expend lives to save us.

###

August 25

August 24 had come and the Iraqis turned up the heat—literally. They attacked the water and electricity. The electricity was easy. It had been turned off just like that, dramatically so, as it had occurred during Howell's introductory speech, a suiting climax to his remarks. The loss of electricity was the signature of their control of us. We still had the generator part-time for the State Department communication system, and as a temporary by-product, the part-time air conditioning system, but the temperature was above 120 most of the day. There was only the briefest relief from the heat.

And we could send messages over the encrypted embassy communication system via satellite when the equipment was turned on with the precious generator power. The exchange of Bible verses between Shirley and me began. We were limited in the length of messages we could send, and the Bible verses designated only by chapter and verse and conveyed information more economically than we could otherwise. But without electricity our lives were altered for the duration, whatever that might be.

The water was a bit more difficult for them. They didn't lick the problem right away. We were told a Palestinian service worker led them astray and took them to the wrong valve, an old one no longer functional. I hoped the poor guy didn't get himself killed over our water.

More journaling to Shirley. *I still have a concept of God's will in this event, which is now painful to me. But if this concept is correct, then we are in for a real time of testing.... I believe God has given you unique strength and faith to be a true testimony in this and the time that follows. I keep thinking of Jim and Elizabeth Elliott. If Jim hadn't died on that beach in Ecuador, Elizabeth's testimony might not have shown forth.... God's plan is the best ... keep telling the little ones about me if I don't return.... Come quickly, Lord Jesus.* My reflections flowed down a masochistic drain. Perhaps such thoughts were a negative view, or maybe they were positive. I didn't know the answer yet.

The Republican Guard troops were gone, leaving the poor draftees to fend for themselves in the sweltering heat. The lower-echelon Iraqi soldier got little or no support from their officers. We saw their bread truck come round every few days, but it was not a regular occurrence.

The Iraqi soldiers broke into abandoned houses to forage what they could. Before the invasion, Barbara had rented a house just down the block from the embassy. Everyone said, "Barbara, just stay here in the embassy. Forget the house." But our instructions had little force. She made trips to her house periodically and found evidence of the troops' thievery. She shouldn't have ventured out, but she was determined to do it her way. She still had the self-assurance of the immune diplomat.

August 27

I got your message today with the Proverbs citation. Since technicians who transmit the messages may or may not know the Bible and the Scripture references, it's hard to be sure about their accuracy.

FAITH IN CRISIS

The message I got read Proverbs 3, 5, and 6. I knew what you meant (Proverbs 3:5, 6). Verse 5 struck home: "Trust in the Lord with all your heart, and do not lean on your own understanding." I had no choice but to follow those instructions. Lord, how much longer will you restrain us ... I know we've been given so much. We don't deserve any more. Nevertheless we ask for your help, Lord, more help.

###

More details came about those who departed in the convoy a few days earlier. Over dinner by the pool we heard the news from Gale Rogers, code name Gazelle, the new embassy consul. Like several others in the embassy trap, Gale had arrived just before the invasion and found herself with a much different job than she anticipated. "The Iraqis in Baghdad let the women and children go. Instead of the plane flight we hoped for them, they sent them out by land vehicles departing Iraq over the northwestern land route via Mosul toward Zakho and Turkey. But they kept the older males, even the teenage boys. It looks like they're going to have to stay in the US embassy in Baghdad." But we finally knew for sure the children on the convoy got out. Praise the Lord for that gift. Now that the women and children were returning to the US, Shirley should get some phone calls from the women.

We belabored ourselves with the paranoid fear the diplomatic corps in the Kuwait embassy would "sell us out." Surely we were worth something in a trade. This fear was not based on any fact, but all we had to do was worry and think about the worst that might occur.

The phone lines were still intact. Why would the Iraqis allow open phone communication? Perhaps they listened in. Or maybe it was just ineptitude. But we were grateful to be able to keep in touch with our friends stuck out in the community. Many didn't have enough food, and we derived secret pleasure from the fact they were worse off than we were.

August 28

We still were blessed by having water. We didn't know how the Iraqis could have failed to close it off. Pretty unimpressive engineers, I guess. We knew they'd get it eventually.

###

The ambassador was committed to staying as long as possible and he made every effort to assure us of his commitment to us. "I know you're all worried about what the plan here is for everyone. We're doing everything possible to make sure we can stay here together. But we have to work together to make this work. And this is no longer a democracy. I'm in charge and there'll be no votes." He wanted to make certain we knew the score, and he was more than able to get his message across. "And with the many departures, we have enough supplies to survive many months. It could take a long time for this to play out, but we're in this together." We all hoped for a rapid conclusion, but once the vast troop movements began, it could take more time than we ever thought.

The military guys in the group, notably Felipe, were pessimistic about a quick resolution. "It'll take months to get several hundred thousand troops and equipment into position, and they'll never go against the Iraqi army unless our force is large enough for certain victory." The news said the Iraqis had 265,000 troops in the country.

Why should the US go to the trouble of putting the Al-Sabahs back in power? But it was only the oil that mattered. More than half the US oil supply came from Kuwait and the Middle East. We had to have their supply. Thank the Lord for the oil he put in the ground. The oil was the reason we might be safe.

August 29

We could still see TV programs from time to time. All the Saddam programs on TV showing the hostages didn't bother me. It was good for us the American hostages were paraded before the public, and the folks in the US could get the right idea about Saddam. Those displays made Saddam look foolish in his misunderstanding of their appearance on international news. One of the videos showed Saddam with a group of "guests." One was a little British boy he tried to treat as sort of a surrogate grandchild. The video of his greeting the frightened little boy was priceless to our cause. The more bad publicity Saddam created for himself, the better the preparation of the American people for war. What a selfish thought, but there it was. CNN made certain we were always in the news.

Our daydreams, despite the surrounding soldiers, were about a variety of topics, but mostly escape routes—overland, by the sea, helicopter rescues.

But there was much to be thankful for. The group of believers on the compound remained small but solid. We prayed for the salvation of others here, especially since they might not have another chance.

###

The diplomatic staff informed me I was on the payroll as a physician at $2900 a month—not much, but better than the nothing I was earning. The Kuwait government cancelled our contracts effective the day of the invasion, or so I had heard. I hoped I fixed it so State Department money would get to Shirley. I sure didn't need it in the embassy. The only currency on the compound was our good behavior and what we could contribute to the enterprise.

I thanked the Lord I felt healthy and strong. I ate everything possible and took vitamins. I should have shared the store of vitamins in the infirmary but I didn't, except for vitamins with iron for the women—my attempt at chivalry. My weight held at 64–65 kilograms. I wanted to be as strong and fat as possible if we were compelled to go to another location that was less advantageous. If Saddam took us, we wouldn't get much food. My GI tract was surprisingly good, no diarrhea or abdominal pain. Usually my intestines were the first of my body to go in adversity. I asked God for strength for all here. Not all were as well off as I was.

After a couple of tries over the course of several days, the Iraqis finally conquered the plumbing mystery. Our city water supply was off. Thank God we had the large storage tanks filled with water, which we estimated would last many months. No more showers. No problem: having lived in Kuwait for quite a while, I was pretty immune to body odors.

August 30

The atmosphere was good on the compound, but the attitude of the residents fluctuated daily and even within the course of the day. We were up, we were down. Or maybe it was just me who oscillated. There was no rationale for either hope or despair. A little word on the news could tip the scale in either direction.

But we lost ground. The air conditioning availability decreased. The fuel had to be conserved to preserve the use of the embassy communication system. As much as I wanted the AC, I didn't want to lose touch with the US and the State Department.

The temperature neared 130 degrees in the afternoon. I had often wondered how the Bedouins survived in the desert. I found out. The answer was simple: *you just do.* You either decide to

FAITH IN CRISIS

survive or you do not. Activities requiring physical activity were accomplished in the morning. Midday was for sleeping or mental activity. The evening was for awakening to life and some form of pleasantry, if it could be found.

We were still a lot better off than the desert Bedouins. We had the pool. I couldn't picture my Bedouin friends ever going for a swim. As we paddled around in the pool in the afternoons, the Iraqi officer corps looked down on us from the hotel balconies towering over us. We were the truly privileged Americans, sunning and vacationing in a war zone. The continual irony of the Iraqis peering down on us enjoying ourselves by the pool in the evenings was a source of quiet enjoyment. Who was really trapped here? Were we or were they?

I was sorry for the Westerners out in the community. The only communication they had was the local phone line. The Iraqis were still picking up Westerners, but the numbers taken were small. Either the Iraqis weren't trying or they weren't good at it.

The city continued to be looted extensively. A friend phoned from the outside and said their apartment building had been cleaned out—doorknobs, toilet fixtures, sinks, anything removable. I don't know how they'd survived. I'm sure their reports were true because we'd observed the huge lorries roll by the embassy on Gulf Road. Much of what they were hauling would be considered junk in any other venue.

I know all the children are growing up through this, thanks to you and God's care for them. The experience is humbling to me. I know I needed that.... May God grant you continuing grace and faith.... I'm not essential to anything.

The ambassador had done a great job of stocking the larder of the embassy. The freezers were full—tons of dressed turkeys.

JIM AND SHIRLEY CARROLL

Thus, the experiment began. How long could turkeys stay frozen and suitable for consumption with no electricity and daytime temperatures above 120? As the doctor, I was asked to participate in making decisions on food spoilage, another part of my medical training that had been ignored. We had to err on the side of safety. Muffled explosions in the freezers signaled the turkeys' demise. Who would have known a turkey could explode? Had this experiment ever been conducted previously? Their interment took place in the garden. I wondered if the burial crew would find the dogs we had entombed earlier.

The fate of the frozen food was decided. An attempt at drying the remaining meat failed. We used as much of the food as possible before we decided it was no longer safe to eat. Sure there was disappointment at the food's passing, but there were rows and rows of canned food in the stores and all the rice we'd ever want. And the canned tuna was choice—Tongol, white meat tuna from Thailand—maybe 6000 cans. All the tomato paste in the world was at our disposal.

The engineers among the American citizen group did a miraculous job keeping the embassy running. They rerouted wiring and redid the plumbing, resurrecting enough toilets to handle the traffic. There was a glorious plywood outhouse constructed in the side yard midway between the residence and the wall. It was located over an inlet into the sewer line. *Playboy* magazines were strategically placed by the toilet seat, another unintended gift from the departing Marines.

###

At this point there were still a few children left in the embassy. Some families had sent their children out with "official" adoptions with the adults who departed. Pastor Maurice and his wife couldn't part with their two boys and had elected to stay together.

FAITH IN CRISIS

Our numbers were gradually shrinking with the departure of those considered disabled, as allowed by the Iraqis. Besides the eight diplomatic staff remaining, the number of citizens would gradually fall to nineteen. Ambassador Howell was mindful of his responsibility to maintain order among the group not accustomed to taking orders in a semi-military setting. For the safety of all, he had to keep control over nondiplomats who were not yet integrated into the chain of command system that was necessary for all in the embassy.

After the initial introduction by Howell on the way things would have to be, an opportunity for an object lesson came on the scene. A short wave radio was available in the compound but was declared off limits for use by nondiplomatic personnel. While the embassy phone system was widely used by all, the Iraqis could interpret the short wave radio use as carrying special messages. For us to use the radio, even for chatting with other Westerners around the town, might be dangerous because the Iraqis were monitoring communications on short wave. Thus we were informed about the reason for the radio being forbidden. The Iraqis might misinterpret what was said and take some unanticipated action. We were instructed to avoid the short-wave set.

The ambassador discovered the radio had been exploited by a couple of the guys. How could he have known? The ambassador was a big, powerful-looking man, with a Moses-like white beard, and this was an opportunity for him to employ his physical presence. He appeared on the scene where most of us were gathered about the pool, strangely good-timing, and he raised the radio over his head and carried it out among us inmates. His face was red with distended veins. The radio was large and probably quite heavy. There in the middle of us he smashed the radio onto the cement. The fragments splattered, reminiscent of Moses smashing the Ten Commandments. "I told you the radio couldn't be used. I meant what I said. Somebody's going to get us killed for no reason. We're in a dangerous situation."

The spectacle proved effective in demonstrating his authority and convincing us we had to accept his rules. I couldn't tell if his display of anger and controlled violence were spontaneous or for show. I suspected the latter. Anyway he proved his point. He sustained a laceration on one finger with the little show. Howell was visibly tired from his display, and the little crowd melted away. I dressed the wound. I was glad I was not one of the perpetrators.

Chapter 6

Others Got Out, I Didn't

August 31

How did Reverend Jesse Jackson get into Kuwait? If we couldn't get out, how could Jesse get in? Was this gesture another Saddam trick, with poor Jackson as the pawn, one that was designed to show how peaceful little Kuwait, the new province of Iraq, actually was? Jackson's trip was billed as a goodwill visit to rescue hostages. He and his news entourage group appeared at the back gate of the embassy with an Iraqi minder and the vice consul from the US embassy in Baghdad. The spectacle and the presence of someone come to help was briefly uplifting, but I began to feel like an actor in a choreographed play.

Jackson was not formerly in my list of American heroes, but the fact he came elevated him into that group as far as I was concerned. No other such interveners appeared at our doorstep. Jackson's first visit was apparently to obtain a list of those who needed to go.

JIM AND SHIRLEY CARROLL

He wasn't allowed to enter the compound, and the relevant discussion occurred over the turnstile that had been chained. I wondered who had put on the chain: the Iraqis or the embassy staff? Probably the latter, as a visual indication to the Iraqis that we were still sovereign. The group in the embassy crowded around the gate and I couldn't get near enough to listen to the exchange, but I understood the ambassador argued for the release of the children and anyone who had a believable medical situation. If I had been prepared, I could have composed a plausible proof of medical need. I was glad for Jackson's courage and the release of a number of our membership. But why did the Iraqis give him special privilege?

Still there was my jealousy about my not being one of those released. But given the Iraqis' recurring duplicity, there was no certainty any of it would turn out for good. The men with illnesses might still be retained in Baghdad.

Jackson returned the next day just as he had promised, having gotten permission to take out the group. He was able to collect several men from the community to be released because of age or various physical difficulties. Odessa Higgins and her husband were included in the group, and they had been discharged from the hospital especially for this purpose. The Iraqis were probably glad to rid themselves of any responsibility for her care. All told, there were perhaps twenty—including some who had not been in the compound—who got out with Jackson. One was my former "pain in the butt" friend, and I was glad for him. I didn't know any of the others who had qualified for release. Jackson shouted for all to hear, "Let us bow our heads to the Lord and ask for His blessing. Join hands!" He then proceeded with a long prayer I couldn't hear. All around obediently bowed.

I wish I could have been among the medical evacuees. Of all the Americans who might come to pull off the same deal, Jackson was the only one to come through. If he came back again, I resolved to be ready with some kind of illness cooked up. As good as the transaction was for those who got out, it was another downer for me. We were better off with a smaller number on the compound, but my jealousy reigned.

I began to work on concocting some kind of believable illness—you'd think a doctor could figure it out. I had been seeing a few spots in my visual field, probably a migraine phenomenon again. But I recalled my eye doctor back in the States had noted a spot on my retina that "needed to be watched." Maybe the spots signaled a retinal detachment, certainly a "medical emergency." Could I sell this idea? It was in my mind as an alternative at some point, one that never materialized. The pseudo-illness was just one of a number of escape plans that served mainly as fantasy or entertainment.

And then the word was that more women and children, medical cases, and Arab Americans might be released. The Iraqis followed a disorganized and therefore tantalizing pathway in deciding who was to be released. The path extended over subsequent weeks, but none of the designated releases included men like me. Left behind again.

###

I was still a hostage, and the embassy was my home for the time. Sure there were events accruing to the positive, but unless we were released they counted for little.

The humidity came on off the sea the night after Jackson's visit. The water condensed on the roofs and flowed off like a rain shower. Even having lived several years in Kuwait, I had seen nothing like it. I went out for a swim in the pool, and upon getting out I found I couldn't dry off. The AC ran only four hours a day to conserve fuel, and the heat and humidity marched on.

While Jackson had succeeded in his mission, Perez De Cuellar (UN Secretary General) continued some kind of negotiation, but the info was fuzzy UN stuff as far as I was concerned. Was it the usual UN face-preserving ritual? I recalled De Cuellar's unsuccessful intercession in the Contadora peace effort in Central America and his negotiations over the Falklands Islands conflict between Argentina and Great Britain, a war the Argentine writer Jorge Luis Borges referred to as "a fight between two bald men over a comb." We had little shared confidence in De Cuellar and the UN to solve our dilemma.

The report of atrocities in the community came to us soon after. Whenever a resistance fighter was captured, their families were murdered, even the children. What a peculiar word, "atrocity." It was awful and spectacular in its meaning yet impersonal. You think of bad things but there's no subjective or personal connection. If only half the reports were true, we knew it would be hard for the world to overlook them. The more this news got rolling, the harder for Saddam and the Iraqis to extract themselves and save face.

The Iraqis took medical equipment from the hospitals, resulting in inadequate treatment of Kuwaiti patients. I heard from friends in the medical community that Iraqi academics from Baghdad had come down to the medical school and the Kuwait Institute for Scientific Research to pick out the equipment they could use in their labs. The medical school library was stripped of its volumes. I wondered what happened to the pitiful door attendant we had encountered at the medical school during our one visit in the early days of the invasion.

Saddam was staying for all he could get, and he couldn't just pick up and leave. He would lose face. Westerners don't get the idea of "saving face." For us it's "Let's just forget it and move on, no one will remember anyway." And they don't. For an Arab saving face is an honor thing, a thing that will never go away, a thing involving not only the individual but also the extended family, the whole people group. And everyone remembers.

Saddam couldn't just pick up and go home. The legend of Saladin would plague him.

The looting was unbelievable. Day after day huge flatbed trucks rolled by with goods of all kinds—food, furniture, new cars, old cars, bathtubs, doorknobs, virtually everything except the building structures themselves. Much of what they took we would consider junk. The Iraqis cleared out entire apartment buildings by kicking in the doors and evicting or capturing the occupants. Then they brought in trucks and loaded everything. They removed bathroom fixtures and even the wiring.

Chapter 7

One Month Anniversary and the Arab Roof

September 2

Last night there was gunfire all around the compound with tracer bullets overhead in random patterns. The night sparkled. Was this a planned show of some kind? Why the fireworks? The two private citizens in the compound who knew a lot about military weapons spoke up in explanation. They were reluctant to share their personal data and the source of their knowledge, but not the knowledge itself. We hung on to their information.

From them I learned what tracers are. Tracers are bullets with a small pyrotechnic charge in their base. When the bullet is fired, the pyrotechnic burns brightly, like a firecracker, making the trajectory visible. This brightly visible bullet enables the shooter to make aiming corrections without using the sights of the weapon. About every fifth bullet fired from an automatic weapon may be a tracer. Perhaps the nighttime tracer show from the assault rifles indicated that the Kuwait resistance was picking up steam or maybe it was just taking note of the one-month anniversary of the invasion. We could only guess the source.

Where did the light show originate? Likely from the roofs of the homes. The roof of an Arab house is often flat and accessible by the occupants. The picture of the rooftop brought to my mind was David spying out Bathsheba from his rooftop to hers. As September 2 was the one-month anniversary of the invasion, Kuwaiti women mounted their house roofs during the day around prayer time and shouted "Allahu Akbar!" along with ululations, which were produced by moving the tongue back and forth rapidly in the roof of the mouth, along with emitting a high-pitched utterance. The sound reverberated among the walls of the closely placed houses. Ululations required practice and were hard for the uninitiated to imitate. The effect of the musical, repetitive notes and rifle volleys was magical and inspiring. The Iraqis responded with full force in combating the resistance. We didn't know the outcome of the battle, if it was fair to call it a battle.

I had acquired a little experience by that time with the sounds of combat, as limited as they were from our vantage point. Pretty exciting. I had spent my Navy days during the Vietnam War sequestered in Bethesda Naval Hospital, a cushy assignment to say the least. I guess they took one look at me and decided—*We're not sendin' him.* Prior to Kuwait, I had no experience with the sounds of battle.

The gunfire marking the one month invasion had an odd effect on me. It was uplifting rather than scary. Of course, I knew it wasn't directed at me. The sounds of battle, either near or the distant artillery fire we heard every so often, had an exhilarating effect. If there was conflict, perhaps there was a resolution coming—that was why I got excited when there was gunfire. The days with no change, no excitement, were the killers for me.

FAITH IN CRISIS

September 3

I pray you're not discouraged. Although things look bad, I'm not too down. I believe I'll eventually get out of this. Don't forget me. I try to hold on to the memory of you and the children. I don't want them to grow up without me.

###

The air conditioner was off all the time. The afternoons were the worst. I had all I could take with sleeping inside in the heat with no AC, so I made the decision to move outside for the first time last night. I carried a single bed mattress up three flights of stairs and placed the mattress on the roof of the Marine barracks. Thanks again to the Lord for the centuries-old Arab rooftop. I wondered how many Marines had preceded me to that same spot.

My friend Joe joined me. Joe and I spent a lot of time talking on the roof before we went to sleep. Joe had white hair and a white moustache. He was thin like me. He had an attractive, gravelly voice. Joe and his friend, Al, had arrived in Kuwait just a day before the invasion. "We were just coming up to Kuwait for a little vacation. We wanted to get out of Saudi a while. It was suffocating there. We called up to Kuwait and arranged a fishing boat for a couple of days on the Gulf. When we crossed into Kuwait, I thought the border guards down at Nuwaseeb seemed a little surprised about our entry. But we didn't think much about it. They probably knew it was bad time to enter Kuwait."

Joe's mention of Nuwaseeb called back memories of glorious afternoons in the soft sand and under the palm trees at the Nuwaseeb beach with Abdullatif and his family at their cottage. Putting the first toes into the water produced not even the slightest shock: the warm sea was that pleasant. And the water was shallow enough to wade out several hundred yards, watching the little fish nibbling our feet all the while. When the sun set, we barbecued, usually chicken, in the fading light. If we ate fish, the servants brought baked hamour wrapped in foil from the little restaurant nearby. Hamour is a general term for several species of Gulf reef fish, all flaky and sweet.

But the memories of those times were eclipsed. The Iraqis had probably already trashed the beach house.

Joe and his friend stayed at a local hotel in the city and after the first night, the Iraqis invaded. "We were completely surprised. There were other Americans and Brits in the hotel, and none of us had any idea what to do. I thought we oughta get out of the hotel, make a run for it and try to get back to Saudi, or maybe come to the embassy. We stalled around for a day. Al was no help. He ignored the whole thing, said he had to go wash his clothes. His escape from Kuwait was to escape from reality. I realized I'd made the trip with the wrong guy." Joe and I wore ourselves out talking about Kuwait, Saudi, and the Iraqis, what mistakes we'd made getting ourselves into this.

The breeze off the sea after midnight was lovely, and I almost needed a blanket. We could look out over the city—few lights, no movement due to the curfew, no cars. Gulf Road should have been busy with shoppers and those who chose to walk by the sea. Joe waxed starry-eyed about the appearance of the city. "Altogether a strange thing, a big city, totally quiet, no lights, no people, no movement."

Joe was a former Air Force navigator having served in Vietnam. I got free astronomy lessons. With the now minimal light from the city and the clear desert air, the stars were unbelievable. How could I even question whether God was in charge?

What about my friend Joe? He was a sixty-two-year-old man who was visiting Kuwait during the invasion. He had been working on contract as an English teacher in Saudi Arabia for Aramco Oil after his wife died a year or so before. I gathered he had been depressed and lost after his wife's death, and sought out

FAITH IN CRISIS

an escape in Saudi to set his mind straight again. He had been in Saudi teaching English as a second language and had decided to take a trip with his friend up to Kuwait.

Joe taught me how to find the North Star. You line up the two stars on the dipper side of the Big Dipper. Then you follow that line down to the North Star. With that single piece of information, we always knew the direction of true north.

Could we use Joe's skills to leave the embassy and make it to Saudi Arabia? The night dreams of escape began. If we could just get over the wall and the razor wire and onto the beach, we could steal a small boat and head out over the Gulf to the US fleet that must be just over the horizon. We could see boats still tied up by the dock on the other side of the road. Then there was the question whether the gas tanks on the outboards would have any gasoline in them. We might make it even with oars if the sea was with us. The Iraqi sentries, at least some of them, frequently slept on guard duty. Their supervision was minimal, and we rarely saw their officers. I could picture us sneaking by the poor recruits. Boy, would they be in trouble.

Or perhaps we could get out over the desert by traveling only at night, thus avoiding the Iraqi troop emplacements. We snooped around in one of the vacant offices and found all sorts of great stuff—photos of the mujahedeen around a campfire in Afghanistan, with their Russian rifles likely lifted from the bodies of their enemies, all kind of maps, a veritable treasure of information, nothing really important, but maybe left by the CIA on the compound. Our speculations on the significance of the various objects heightened their dream value. Any knowledge, any information was a prize, even if it had no real value to our potential escape. But more related to our making a run for it, we found detailed maps of the desert with geographic landmarks and depictions of the types of sand. Of course, we never used them.

JIM AND SHIRLEY CARROLL

The distance to the Saudi border was about seventy miles. Even if we could make fifteen miles a day traveling by night and navigating by the North Star, it would take us more than four days total. There was no way we could carry enough water for that time. Yes, it occupied our minds to make up fanciful escape plans—if only we could get over the razor wire and the sentries were asleep. But the weeks I spent there on the roof with Joe were the best, the sanest part of the whole experience. There was a peace there that was present nowhere else on the compound, except perhaps early morning guard duty, or reading by car battery light late into the night.

Joe and I had a plan for the trip to Baghdad if it was imposed on us by an Iraqi incursion into the embassy. The road would take us up through Basra. Surely we would make a stop there for refueling and maybe a bathroom visit. If so, we'd get out of the vehicle together, head east to the Shatt Al-Arab, steal a small boat and cross over to Iran. Certainly the Persians would be happy to help us since we had escaped from their enemies, the Iraqis. I don't recall how serious we were, probably we didn't even know then.

Joe and I talked into the late hours under the stars. We went to bed too late and rose tired. But it was worth it.

The flies zoomed in faithfully every morning at 5:15 and we were awakened to sunrise across the Gulf.

Chapter 8

Things Fall Apart

As things fell apart in Kuwait and in our small estate of the embassy, my mind went to Chinua Achebe's African novel of the same name. I couldn't get the title out of my head. As things fell apart here—the electricity, the water, our communications, our food, the rules had to change, too. The social structure tipped over. We, the all-powerful Americans, were wasting away, and we possessed no resource to rectify our situation. I hoped those who remained, the neediest among us, could get out soon. Surely if Jesse Jackson could assist some of the people to get out with various medical problems, other US or British luminaries could come to Kuwait and do the same. The thought of those women and children still trapped in the embassy made me think of my own charges.

I pray for you, John, Peter, Ruth, Rebecca, Timothy, Matthew, and Lydia, that God will give you strength and courage ... I love you. Once more I thanked the Lord Shirley and the children weren't here.

JIM AND SHIRLEY CARROLL

September 4

Kuwait seemed deserted. The population of the city, at least a million normally, must have declined to a few hundred thousand. No one knew for sure, and the Iraqis weren't up for a census yet. I looked out from the top of the Marine barracks. No one was in the streets, no cars, and no pedestrians, only an occasional pair of Iraqi soldiers walking their nighttime beat. Little more than a month ago, even with the normal summer departures, Gulf Road was full of cars, the beach teeming with adults and children, some dangling their feet in the shallows, and even couples holding hands in the darker corners.

The Kuwait Towers were several blocks to our left, easily seen from the roof of the Marine barracks. One of the towers had a large cavity opened by an artillery round. There was no military value in shooting at the towers, but the towers symbolized Kuwait itself. The value of the Towers' bombardment was political humiliation of the Kuwaiti government and people.

Reports coming out of southern Iraq were grisly. Bangladeshis, Indians, Thais, all manner of Asians who tried to get out were stranded in the desert due to abandonment by their transporters. They had come to Kuwait to work in hopes of sending money home. Many died, so we were told, but the reports couldn't be counted on.

I recalled Shirley's fears when she took the children out in the desert with the Bedouins. If water or means of travel became unavailable, death was always just a few hours away in the dehydrating heat. Would the accurate numbers of those who died ever be known? But in the midst of war, as I learned, information was muddled, purposely exaggerated, inaccurate, cooked up for effect, or just silly reflections, like the ones we made with our escape plans. If I had believed what I heard about this or that

FAITH IN CRISIS

method of getting out of Kuwait over the desert, I would surely have been captured or died of thirst and heat.

###

We're still expecting the remaining women and children to be evacuated. We needed them out. The real danger for us all was that something unexpected would happen and then violence would break loose. The Iraqi soldiers surrounding us would probably be of little value against an opposing military force, but they might not have sufficient discipline to show restraint against civilians. There was certainly the means available for disaster. And I was afraid the embassy was an obvious focal point.

Despite our being surrounded by maybe half a million enemy soldiers, there was a party attitude in the embassy. We did our best at little jokes at Happy Hour and the dinner following.

"How many UN negotiators does it take to change a lightbulb?"

"Three—one to put in the new bulb, and two to decide whether to turn the light on or off."

"How many diplomats does it take to reach an agreement?"

"There is no answer. This is not possible."

The jokes were bad, but tuned to the moment. Such was our main defense against our falling apart. Everyone tried for the better joke, which was a defense against reality. I suppose the jocularity was to be expected, but my pessimism conflicted with the communal mood. Was the joviality a sign of our societal breakdown?

There were about thirty-five of us on the compound at that point—a mixed group—engineers of all kinds, diplomatic personnel, teachers, the preacher and his wife and two boys, a couple of guys who said they sold arms to whatever country would buy. I'm not sure I believed the self-identified arms traders. Maybe they were just having fun with a story or covering up something else. But they did seem to know a lot about weaponry, enhancing the discussion about the armaments that faced us outside our wall.

"There goes another T-55."

Every morning for several weeks we heard disturbing gunfire, and the sounds were occurring within a few blocks of the compound. Always at 8:00 AM there were several volleys of rifle fire, with all shots fired simultaneously. It was definitely not target practice, and it was not the resistance. The shooting was limited and too regular. The image evoked in our minds by the sounds was of a firing squad. Here was another source of unpleasant speculation. Who were the victims? Would we be subject to the same if the Iraqis came in?

September 5

It's 6:00 AM and I've finished Bible study. I am filled with thankfulness for all we have—the children, our life together, so many material things—really all we've ever asked for. God hasn't failed us yet. Why should he this time...? I love you so much.

Remember how we wondered at the Iraqi attempts to rebuild Babylon and how we wanted to go up and see it for ourselves? It's hard to believe there was a time when we could have gone and actually seen the project. At that time travel from Kuwait to Iraq and back was relatively free, just between the states of Arab brothers. It would have been just a day trip for the family.

Maybe this was the chief error of the Iraqis—look at Jeremiah 50:39a, "Therefore wild beasts shall dwell with hyenas in Babylon, and ostriches shall dwell in her," and Isaiah 13:19-20a, "And Babylon, the glory of kingdoms, the splendor and pomp of the Chaldeans, will be like Sodom and Gomorrah when God overthrew them. It will never be inhabited or lived in for all generations." I have no claim over understanding prophecy though. It's enough that God knows.

We had prayer meeting many nights, and five or six adults attended. Some attended but didn't pay attention. Why did they come? Several in the meeting were openly antagonistic. It convinced me we didn't wage war against the forces of men but against the evil one and his demons.

Walk by faith, so the Scriptures say. Do we have any other choice…? A month ago I was struggling with the idea of faith—particularly in regard to the faith I saw in Suhair's mother. Now I'm confident the object of the faith is the most important factor. Somehow the walk is little easier, perhaps because there's no other choice. It's an ambivalent condition—being anxious because of what might be ahead, and at the same time having no alternative other than what God has placed in front of me—that's faith by the imposition of God. I'm starting to see there's no other faith than the one God imposes on me.

###

September 6

The confusion continued. When would the women and children be released? The indication of their potential release had been conveyed to the ambassador though Iraqi military channels, but the Iraqis' communications were confused and contradictory. The working out of the details sauntered along, and there was no reliable mechanism for getting them to the departure points. The Iraqis were confused about how to handle it. The muddle, I considered, was the standard for an occupying force. And there had been another Iraqi error: an American was shot two days ago, but we couldn't learn of his location or any details. The Iraqis were trying to cover the matter, but our risk rose.

I know John's birthday is coming soon. It's hard to believe he'll be twenty-one. He's been a joy. I know I've not done my best for him and have not been totally fair. I pray he will not take those affronts with him. He is so forgiving, never a harsh word about anyone. God is with him. I pray for him that he will be God's man.

I somehow feel I've been fairer with Peter. I pray for his toughness, that it will be converted to a tender, loving heart.... We've already seen signs of Peter's gentle heart with Rania recently. I pray God will give him the self-control so that God may use him.

With Saddam, there is no element of morality, but rather cruelty, dishonesty, and no regard for human life, this endless, ridiculous search for power. There is every indication he is a man of great iniquity. He will not die of old age.

September 7

Today the first plane of women and children were scheduled to leave. I knew I should be happier for them. But why not me? I was still thankful for the chance to assist with the evacuations of the women with children who were US citizens because they were born in America.

Last night there was another firefight around the compound. They were using small arms, and no bullets came over the substantial compound wall and into the compound. If they had used mortars, we would have been in trouble. The Kuwaiti resistance likely provoked the fight. Not very effective, but it was good to know they were still active.

Every night around the evening meal there is a time of joking and gaiety—the same stories over and over, our main defense against the truth. I didn't take much part in it. I was aware it was because I felt spiritually superior. Or maybe it was because I had a more accurate view of reality. Or maybe it was just because I was a stick.

I am now convinced the spiritual reality takes precedence over the material reality. Perhaps it's more accurate to say they are one and the same. Create in me a clean heart, Lord.

As Achebe wrote, *"Things fall apart."*

Chapter 9

Depression Sets In

September 8

Six in the morning. I was on guard duty at the back gate beyond the parking area, and the Iraqi sentries on the other side of the wall were dozing. I had been in the embassy compound only a little more than three weeks and the constant threat of unexpected, undesired change was wearing on me. Guard duty was always a little nerve-wracking because of the possibility the Iraqis might choose to enter the compound exactly at the time of my duty. The back gate guard post was at the farthest point in the compound from the rest of inmates. And because I was far from the others, I was in a heightened sense of alertness. But as the days moved on, the likelihood of their entering diminished. If they were going to come in and get us, they should have invaded earlier. All in the compound slowly relaxed over the lessening likelihood of their entry, except, of course, for guard duty.

JIM AND SHIRLEY CARROLL

There was minimal physical risk on guard duty. We were told not to resist if the Iraqis tried to enter. Our only responsibility was to inform the communication center if there was an incursion. A little time would be needed for those in the communication area to destroy the encryption equipment. The purpose of its destruction was to prevent the Iraqis from getting into our code and computer system. But from what we saw, it was unlikely they would be able to make any sense of it. After all, they had trouble turning off the embassy's water faucet.

I sat there looking at the US flag flapping the breeze. Its presence was an affront to the Iraqis that we were holding US territory. If they came in, the US response would be required. They didn't want the trouble and therefore they wouldn't come in after me. At least those were the thoughts that protected me for the morning. Such were my judgments, which were able to stave off fear.

But I didn't like being there at the back gate, a good distance from the rest of the camp, because I found it more stressful. I preferred the front gate because I was near the others, and I requested duty there thus avoiding the back gate. And to multiply my concern that morning, the Iraqis were jamming our radio frequency. The radio I had on the guard post was giving out constant static. I had no way to notify the communication encryption center. Was there some plan in their jamming the radio frequency, or were they just practicing their craft?

I covered the duty for Maurice that morning in hopes the Iraqis would allow his wife and children to depart on that day. The Iraqis were unpredictable about arranging any releases. I was thankful I didn't have the same worries about Shirley and the children. I wondered if Shirley would leave me and go back to the US if we were in the same circumstance as the Grahams. I'm afraid if she were here she would have to do the same. The threat of worsening was always present. We didn't know when or if the

FAITH IN CRISIS

Iraqis' policy toward us would be altered to a more aggressive direction. And if this occurred, there was the genuine concern for rape of women.

I couldn't help ruminating over the predicament. It was the Romans 8:28 conundrum again. If God works for the good for those who love him, why should God take me away from seven children, three of whom we adopted? I knew His plan was best, but I didn't get it. I could make no sense of 8:28 here in the embassy in the context of my role as father to seven. I knew I had many faults as a father, but I also believed I had much to give. I thought of Ruth, Rebecca, and Timothy, their need for a father and their nearness to me. Matthew and I had such a special relationship. And Lydia—she won't remember me if it goes on much longer. How will God use this for good? I know he will, but I don't know how.

Shirley, He loves you more than I, though I don't see how that's possible. If He allows me to return, it will be another gift I don't deserve.

September 9

We thought the Iraqis wanted to get rid of some of the hostages as a way to mollify the attitude of the US. But the expectation that the Iraqis would release the women and children on the compound was unmet. Were the Iraqis playing games with our sensibilities, or can they just not get their act together? Or both? Maurice kept his eyes straight ahead and didn't speak or make eye contact.

That morning it struck me the Iraqis didn't plan to stay in Kuwait. I saw they were carting off traffic lights, and they weren't bringing their civilians down to Kuwait. There were plenty of places where their citizens could live—empty villas, apartment houses with floors and floors of vacant dwellings. As far as we knew, most of the captured Westerners have been taken to Iraq, not left as "shields" here in Kuwait.

JIM AND SHIRLEY CARROLL

Even in the early morning at the gate again, the heat oppressed and served to set up my mind for the endless day ahead. As I sat there trying to avoid the sun in my eyes, I strained to come up with a plan for the day, a typical day that required no plan. My actions during the day had no impact. I needed a *raison d'etre*, but there was none, and a hollow feeling resulted.

In the mental and physical downtime, my colleagues and I considered the army that lay in front of us. We concluded that Saddam and his army must be destroyed. And we were in the middle of where we thought the battle would take place. The Iraqis expected the allies' attack to come from the sea, and we were precisely in the spot where the beach landing might occur. We watched the Iraqis train their big guns out toward the sea just across Gulf Road right in front of us. The diplomats suggested there was a plan to protect us when the battle came. I appreciated the sentiment, but how would we get out of here alive? *I am in God's hands. Shirley, I know you are, too.*

September 10

I reflected about Saddam. He gained more attention from us than he deserved. Would he pull back to northern Kuwait and settle for the oil fields there? I was sure the Kuwaitis would settle for that price if he offered.

There was talk continually about the strength of the US forces and about getting us out. The sanctions must be total if they were to work, and I was afraid they're not total. All these thoughts recurred in random and pointless manner. We had nothing to do but think about what might happen.

Meanwhile our food situation was slowly deteriorating—tick-tock our clock was running down. I estimated about a two to three months' supply was left. But we had plenty of rice and pasta and about 6000 cans of tuna.

FAITH IN CRISIS

###

September 11

Last night the alcohol gained the upper hand during and after the Happy Hour. The alcohol consumption reflected the need to hide from reality. One man lost consciousness. His pals discovered him in the early morning unconscious out by the pool on the concrete, and they summoned me to the scene for what might be a medical emergency. Unexplained coma in an adult was a challenge for a neurologist, particularly for a pediatric neurologist. But this was not a tough test. At least he was breathing, and the smell of alcohol was strong. The guys brought me over to him as he lay on his side, his hands supporting his head. One tried to rouse him. "Al, Al, wake up!" But it would take more than a verbal stimulus.

I began to understand what Joe had said about his travel partner: that he could be depended upon to fold at the most inopportune times. I tried to revive Al with the standard medical tests for coma, a few brisk pinches on his nipples and the old reliable sternal rub. He mumbled a bit but didn't get up. The biggest possibility was that he was drunk. But as the physician, I had to reflect on what we call the "differential diagnosis," meaning all possibilities of cause. I considered he might have had a stroke or had developed some sort of coma-producing illness, maybe a diabetic coma, something we couldn't possibly manage on the compound.

His bunkmates were clear, however. "He's just drunk. He's hittin' it all the time. He's got his own stash." From what his friends said, I was pretty sure it was the liquor. I couldn't do any tests to be sure. The pressure was on me to make the right decision in a circumstance of this type. If I misdiagnosed an illness that required hospital treatment, it would be a disaster for poor old Al. And if I said he needed to go to the hospital and it was just an alcoholic binge, then I would have given him to the Iraqis. I thus landed on the diagnosis of "drunk."

After several hours he regained his sensibility, and I laid out the possibilities for him. "Al, if this keeps happening there's nothing good to come from it. If I find you down and I can't be sure what's wrong, I'm gonna have to turn you over to the Iraqis. You won't like that, but you might leave me no choice."

Al straightened himself upright. "No, Doc, don't do that. I'll get control of myself. You'll see. You won't find me here again."

Under Howell's authority Al's quarters were raided, and he was relieved of his ample supplies. Martial law reigned.

Several others had been drinking too much. Their mood on the surface was okay, but underneath we were all the same. Any rational person would have the same fears in the middle of an invasion, and alcohol was a good remedy for free-floating fear. The alcohol supply present in the embassy looked endless. I was certain, however, the ambassador would get control of the alcohol. Even though alcohol is not legal in Kuwait, the US embassy was American soil, an ethanol oasis.

Even in the midst of the alcoholic near-debauch, my mind drifted home for a moment. *Today is John's birthday. I pray for him in all he does.* How many birthdays will I miss?

September 12

Our brief prayer asked God for the safety of the remaining women and children in the compound. The Iraqis kept stalling, or maybe they just couldn't get their orders right from above.

To double up on the worries of the day, we had lost all the food that needed refrigeration. It was gone, and we had to burn it. The turkeys were already in the ground. The temptation was to use the expiring food some way, but the risk was too high. If someone got sick from spoiled food, then they might have to go to Iraqi-controlled hospital system.

And the loss of city water had made things worse. The Iraqis had finally located the correct water line to shut off our external supply. It took them weeks. We still had huge storage tanks of water. As the "doc" it was my responsibility to make sure the water stayed potable. We kept adding chlorine, blah. We had to add excess chlorine to be sure, because we had no way to test its bacterial content other than monitoring for diarrhea occurrences among our residents. And, once again, the torture for Americans—no showers.

Chapter 10

Pain, Self-Inflicted

Towering immediately above us to our right as we faced the sea was the International Hotel. The Iraq officer corps had taken over the hotel. In the evening they got out on their balconies, which looked down on the compound, and lounged like tourists. It was as if we were a source of entertainment for them.

Our relative positions were eccentric. They could see us and we could see them. We, the prisoners, lived better than they, the jailers. We speculated on what they thought about our activities — the maintenance work performed on the compound, the swimming pool activities, the women in Western bathing suits, evening cocktail hour, the communal meal, and evening outdoor movies. These activities continued throughout our time on the compound, and they served as a constant reminder to the Iraqis that we were persisting in spite of them. Were they envious, or did they think we were decadent Westerners? I was sure the word "decadent" had come up, but they envied us nevertheless.

I settled into the evening routine with the others—it was a relief to the thoughts crammed in my head. I drank one or two beers a day while they lasted, mainly for its caloric content. I enjoyed the taste. The liquor was locked up, except at the cocktail time, for the safety of all.

Our thought patterns on the compound were maudlin. We wondered how we would think if we were in Saddam's place. How could he think his gambit might work? From our viewpoint, his actions had no long-term chance of success. But Saddam did not think in Western patterns. Logic failed to predict his next move. His plan seemed to entail a rotation of good cop–bad cop routines all rolled into one. Were we even part of his focal point?

September 13

Our prayers were answered. Yesterday all the women and children were released from the compound. Their departure was a mixed experience, tears plus relief to get out those who might be at risk. It was reprieve for us all to get them out, particularly Maurice. Now that our numbers were down to about thirty, more food and water was available for the rest of us and a little less fretting. Laurie, Maurice's wife, would be able to call Shirley when she gets back to the US. Maurice was sad but relieved to have that responsibility taken care of. We could only pray that they would make it out of Iraq.

With the departures, the concerns expressed in my journal turned to Shirley. My mind lacked sufficient occupation. *I have to tell you at times I can think of nothing besides having sex with you. It has become an obsession. Should I struggle against it…? There has been no one else who has attracted me, now there are only four women left on the compound … I think the sexual obsession is a manifestation of my concentration on my self-inflicted pain.*

FAITH IN CRISIS

I prayed for help to come to Shirley and the family. I had no idea how she was managing, and I knew she wouldn't reveal trouble to me in her messages. I was salved by the report the Kuwaiti government intended to help families financially. Given that my contract had already been cancelled, I would be surprised if they came through.

But I have the constantly recurring fear I will never get out. Why should Saddam ever let the hostages go? The constant thinking and rethinking made my self-imposed low mood even worse.

September 14

You and I are being tried in a holy fire. I don't know God's reasons but I respect them ... Lord, set the captives free. How many times over the centuries has that been said, said by others needier than me? And how many captives have died without physical release ... I pray to be released from this fear and to be given the strength to bear whatever God allows to happen.... Today I've been thinking of Rebecca. I think of her prayers and persistence in them. I think of her prayer for another baby for the family ... I still have not given up hope here, either.... I pray for God to give her grace and understanding beyond her years.

And then to compound the emotional stress, today there was news about the Iraqis taking Western diplomats who had stayed with their embassies. It was hard to know if it was just another rumor, a mistake, or an escalation. If the course continued in that direction, then we were done. We were the biggest and best targets of the bunch. My bet was that it was just a rumor.

September 15

I think the suffering here, the mental not the physical, rived up my spiritual growth. Scripture told me the comparison of what was happening to us in Kuwait paled beside the glory to be had later. When I thought of those before us who have gone through so much more, I felt foolish at my mental complaining. I sensed a responsibility not to complain too much to my hostage colleagues, and I think most shared that feeling.

I am thinking and praying for Timmy this morning. I know he doesn't understand what's going on. He and I were just beginning to develop a relationship. Now, I'm afraid he won't even know me. I pray for his development in the Lord. I know he must need me. But God is enough. I pray Timmy will turn soon to the Lord as his Savior, even as a little child.

Due to all the departures, we revised upward the length of time the supplies will last—probably three to four months. Who's going to give up first? Who's going to act first? Bush or Saddam? Maurice believed Saddam was a paranoid schizophrenic. I thought he was correct. At least Maurice's exercise at long distance psychoanalysis was entertaining.

An assessment of all the personalities involved added up to the situation continuing for a year or more. Neither Saddam nor Bush was willing to lose this one. And if it continues that long, we'll be out of supplies and in Iraq, in some site much less pleasant and accommodating, no swimming pool, no tuna.

I prayed for the other men in custody out in the community. They were in worse shape than we were. We got many calls from them when we were on guard duty. One we heard from lived in the ventilation duct of his apartment building. The Iraqis stripped his building and he was trapped. "The ventilation duct is the only place I feel safe if the Iraqis come back." Several Filipino women took turns bringing food and water to him and his dog. We had no way to confirm any of this. I couldn't blame him if he had created this tale just for drama.

FAITH IN CRISIS

September 16

Maurice talked to me yesterday about suffering. He had identified a theme for me. "Pain has to be felt in your gut, experienced, in order to rise above it. You just have to give in to it to an extent. You can't pretend it's not there. I have to tell you again I'm just sure we're all getting out soon." He was still adopting his counseling role. I didn't think I'd fully gotten the message, but I appreciated his assuming the position without pay.

Many of the others here were able to laugh at jokes and fool around aimlessly during the evening time by the pool. I just didn't understand it, and I didn't fit in. I felt a constant sense of seriousness. Nothing was funny. I don't think Jesus was ever recorded as laughing, and I think I understood. *I remember how I criticized you for your poor sense of humor. I respect that more now.*

September 17

Due to the reported break-in at the French embassy residence, concern over our embassy integrity heightened. Perhaps it was just a rupture in the soldiers' discipline coupled with a lapse in embassy security. But what would our increased security consist of? What point was there in the tightening? The Iraqis could waltz in any time they wanted.

###

Water has reportedly been turned off in parts of the city. What did this mean about the desalinization plants? Maybe the Iraqis were unable to keep them functional. If so, then a population of several hundred thousand citizens, not to mention the thousands of Iraqi soldiers, couldn't be supported. In the old days, water was transported down to the city from the Shatt Al-Arab.

JIM AND SHIRLEY CARROLL

Maybe the water shortage fit in with what we were told about Kuwaitis being allowed to leave via the southern border. At least we heard this. Who knew the truth? If the diplomatic corps had information about such departures, we hadn't been informed.

What sort of information was delivered at the afternoon meetings of the diplomats? We understood they had to meet together for their job. But why were the meeting contents so secret? Was the news that bad? Maybe they feared we'd spill the beans over the phone line and into the community at large, with the Iraqis listening. But what could be so secret that it made a whit of difference?

I have an overwhelming sense of despair. It affects me by immobilizing me and giving me terrible hollow feeling in the pit of my stomach.... If I don't return, I wouldn't want you to know how low, how despairing I am ... but still I'm leaving this for you to read. If I do return and you do read this, well, perhaps we'll both be even more thankful. But the full truth is always best.

Chapter 11

Fleas and Sand in the Tuna, Artillery at Night

September 18

The heat and dust storms made our existence sweaty and grimy. When we lived in our green villa in Jabriya, I had a house-dwellers' appreciation of the dust storms. The dust invaded through the smallest opening. I recall how Shirley and Lena, our housekeeper, persisted in vacuuming the carpet and repeatedly emptying the vacuum of the sand. But from our site on the Marine barracks roof and down by the pool, we had no refuge. The dust was the victor. Shortly after I opened my lunchtime tuna cans and added the barbecue sauce, the grains of sand made the tuna flesh gritty. Fleas and other unidentified insects jumping into the tuna added nourishment.

Our fleas remained as uninvited guests on the compound, perhaps from all the animals here earlier. We were bitten all night long, and it was hard to find a comfortable place to sleep. The roof of the Marine barracks became too windy, dusty, and buggy. What was formerly an oasis became a desert again. Inside, the heat was a real problem, but it was better than the roof. It had been great up there, for a while almost a total escape above the rest of the compound. We hoped the heat and dust would improve in a few weeks.

I'm thankful we could help in getting out many Kuwaiti women and their US-passported children. I suppose I really didn't have much to do with it, but just being there during their evacuation and helping with the phone calls was an upper. If Shirley and the children had been there, I don't know how we could have gotten out Matthew and Ruth, the two of them being obviously Asian. The concept of adoption of that sort was completely foreign to the Iraqis, and they wouldn't have believed they were actually ours. What a mess it would have been.

I was thankful for so much but mostly I felt sorry for myself. If there was some kind of medical evacuation, I wanted to work up a passable excuse to get out. Going to Baghdad was a constant thought on everyone's minds, and I tried to come up with any excuse to avoid it.

September 19

At least there was someone for me to unload on. I talked with Maurice about my feelings of despair. I think it helped a little. It was just that I didn't see any progress in any direction. Maurice assured me we would eventually get out. He was startlingly optimistic, and it had only been six weeks. We were surrounded by several hundred thousand Iraqi troops in what would eventually turn into a battleground. Didn't look so good to me.

In talking with Maurice, I realized we might have trouble if we got home. He was tuned into the psychological effects of the trap we were in. He said it would have longstanding emotional effects on us all. He began to rely on his psychological training to help himself. I denied such thoughts.

I reflected too much on the past, meandering through useless musings. *My work as a physician-scientist seems almost meaningless now. But I know I'm going to have to get organized and come up with some kind of plan for reorganizing what's left of my so-called career. If I ever get out.* Will I ever get back in time for the medical school job in Augusta? How will I reinvent a research career after this? I'll need to depend on the generosity of others. *None of us knows the future and only God can rescue us.* Some were predicting we would be out in two or three weeks. But there was no rational basis for the optimism.

September 20

It was 10:00 AM and only 90 degrees. Maybe the weather was moderating.

Last night there was heavy artillery fire in the distance. The firing made me excited, not afraid. The sounds of battle increased the fantasy that something might happen. I imagined helicopters coming in over the compound walls. Who knows what the firing was about? The Iraqi have no enemies here now in Kuwait who would require heavy artillery. Maybe they were just practicing or testing to make sure their guns still worked. I imagined the accumulation of dust and sand in their gun barrels, perhaps causing the rifling of the barrels to get clogged, thereby diminishing their range and accuracy.

I pray for Matthew's upcoming surgery. And here I am, no help to you. I'm confident in your judgment ... I pray to be with him as he grows up. I want him to be a Godly young man. I want to help deal with his stubbornness and to channel it into the kind of person God would have him to be.

I hear different ideas expressed here as to how this mess may conclude. They are all based on men and machines.... "Some trust in chariots and some in horses, but we trust in the name of the Lord our God." (Psalm 20:7) If we escape from this, people need to be warned that men did not solve the problem, but that God is moving the world to his conclusion. He's slow by our measure, but not by his.

September 21

I am afraid I'm tripping into a genuine depression. I cannot laugh or smile. I awake early in the morning and worry myself into a state of anxiety. The morning is the worst time. I awake when it's dark with worries that don't abate. The daylight heals. I can't read any book except the Bible. The Marine barracks had an extensive library, but it wasn't useful to me yet. *The others around me seem so optimistic, but I see no reason for it. I'm afraid my assessment of the situation is more accurate than theirs. I see two huge armies arrayed against one another. The battle lines form. We're in the middle, of minimal importance to the outcome.... Eventually we will have to go to Baghdad and defeat ... I pray to see you again. I am trying to fight the depression. I pray God will relieve me of it ... I try to keep busy, but there's not enough to do.... I try to keep a thankful heart ... Lord, help me to see what's best here, where I am now.*

September 22

I am obsessed with the idea of getting back to you, but there seems to be little realistic hope now. Bush doesn't want to attack, and I don't blame him. There would be thousands of deaths. Saddam doesn't understand how impossible his situation is. Either we're here for a long time or we face being in the middle of war. We may not survive the fighting.... The fantasy here is one of helicopters coming in over the wall to save us.... As long as I'm in the embassy, you will know what happens to me.... How is

Ruth ... I feel she keeps so much in her mind without talking about what she's thinking. I pray for her, that the Spirit would guide her.

I worried about the passage of messages between us. The responses weren't occurring in a regular fashion. There were so many worries for my mind to turn to. They were always present. *I hope we're being clear with one another. At least the notes of love and Bible verses are getting through.*

Last night there was another round of heavy artillery fire in the distance. The rumblings were felt as much as heard. I hoped something might be happening but after a while the firing stopped. The firing at night was inspiring. We never knew the reason for the shooting, at least so far. If the ambassador knew, he's not telling.

September 23

Although the US and Kuwait are not blameless, and perhaps have even brought this thing on by their own misdeeds, the evil of the Iraqis surpassed anything I've encountered. They were enslaving Pakistanis and Bangladeshis. They refused to let dying men pass through their blockade. Saddam was starving the Vietnamese workers in Iraq. Was there some precursor of the antichrist hiding here?

Could it get worse?

Yes, I suppose it could. The man they installed as the chief of the "Kuwait province" was responsible for gassing the Kurds. And there he was appearing on local TV. Ali Hassan Al-Majid, "Chemical Ali," had ordered the use of mustard gas and sarin against Kurdish targets during the Al-Anfal (The Spoils of War) campaign. The first such attacks occurred in April 1987 and continued into the next year, most notable for the attack on Halabja resulting in the deaths of over 5000 people. This man was certainly up to doing whatever Saddam asked in the subjugation of little Kuwait.

And here we were subject to the same possibility as the Kurds. We didn't know his location, whether he was actually in Kuwait or being televised from Iraq. The choice of Chemical Ali, the guy with the gas, was quite pointed on the part of Saddam. I got the message. He wanted us to know he meant our destruction if we didn't succumb.

I know everyone is praying for me. Don't stop.... Armed conflict is the best alternative to produce peace ... I pray for Matthew's surgery on Tuesday. I don't know how you're managing the finances.

September 24

I received your message about the failure of the Kuwaiti embassy in the US to help. I'm not surprised, but I'm sorry you had to go to the trouble and humiliation of asking them for help.

My mind wandered around among our children. *I think of Lydia now and wonder how she is progressing. I think she is really going to be something. I pray she doesn't forget me. I pray she will know the Lord soon....*

Life here is very dull and routine—the same every day—guard duty, sitting around talking, a swim, a shower with pool water using the bucket technique, eating, a movie, and then bed. I awaken early worrying. The food is adequate for nutrition, but not tasty—I haven't lost weight yet—tuna almost every meal.

September 25

I woke up early this morning. I didn't know the time, because I stopped wearing my watch, which had been rendered a useless instrument. It was still dark, and I knew I wouldn't return to sleep. Just lying there in bed was depressing me, and there didn't seem to be any point to it. It was so quiet, and I waited for the

FAITH IN CRISIS

dawn to break for what seemed like hours. Strangely, I went to sleep quickly in the evening. The bugs weren't as bad now. For a while we were bothered by them continually, probably fleas. My bites were finally healing.

Tensions are building even more as we draw closer to the time when the end of our supplies dictates that we must leave the compound. If the war begins, and it is certain there will be war, while we're in Baghdad, our fate there is unpredictable. We might never get out.

I'm thinking of Peter this morning. I pray he'll continue to learn to control himself. He has so much potential with people—and he has good looks, musical abilities—so many non-Carroll attributes.

September 26

I was heartened this morning. The UN approved the air embargo disallowing any supply of goods and materials to Iraq by air. But in the big picture, this was a minimal effort that accomplished little. What did this blockade really mean for them? How much were they receiving by air? Only a token of goods, and the Iraqis were unperturbed by the passage.

September 27

Tensions continued to rise on the compound. I didn't see how this could continue without some kind of discharge of energy. The nighttime artillery fire blasted out a brief entertainment song for me.

I wonder how John is doing at Covenant College. Is he able to concentrate? Is he able to formulate his plans? I don't see how he can think clearly.... He's such a kind, gentle person.

September 28

There was confidence among the group this would be over by the end of October. There was a clear intention among the inmates to be as optimistic as possible. I couldn't share, and I saw no reason to expect that date to be true. We never heard the military buffs on the compound come up with such predictions. They understood the technical aspects of moving several hundred thousand allied troops and equipment into position. We understood our troop preparations were in process and that our only intention was war, unless Saddam backed down and departed Kuwait.

My routine was up at 6:00 AM, Bible reading and writing in my journal to Shirley, a little talk with the others, guard duty from 9:00 to 12:00, lunch, Arabic from one to two (it was Moroccan Arabic, quite different from Gulf Arabic, but a diversion), Maurice and I talk and pray from one to two, several laps running around the compound, a swim in the pool, then killing time until dinner. Then the time for uplifting socialization around the pool—at least a distraction.

Chapter 12

Happy Hour

Happy Hour persisted with drinks and jokes for all. There was an abundance of alcohol in the embassy, now locked up for everyone's protection except for the evening and conserved for the long hall. My taste for Scotch whiskey, acquired in Navy days in the early seventies, was reactivated. The Scotch was great tranquilizer and even a mood elevator, and for a time I felt better. But I had to be careful.

At 6:00 PM we gathered around the pool for drinks and conversation. For a few minutes we didn't feel like hostages. We sat down around the umbrella tables for dinner at seven following the Happy Hour and ate in groups of four to six. I ate to guard my weight. I feasted heartily the first round, took a full plate, waited until the others finished, not to be greedy, and then went back to get more. Sergio said, "Boy, can that little guy eat!" I even enjoyed the food at times; it provided a detour from my desert musings. And I was preserving my weight in case we were sent where there was inadequate nutrition. My training in pediatrics kicked in for my personal nutrition analysis. I calculated I needed two tins of tuna each day to satisfy my protein requirement of one to two grams per kilogram per day.

We had a movie video after dinner by the pool. The gasoline generator powered the big TV and video machine between the pool and the multipurpose building to the side. We all knew it wasn't conserving of the gasoline, but the ambassador felt it was a good morale investment. The video assortment from the Marine barracks was endless—*The Alamo, Driving Miss Daisy, The Great Escape,* and on the fifty-sixth day of the embassy closure, *Fifty-Five Days in Peking.* Soon we would hold the record for the longest siege of an American embassy in US history, a source of dubious pride. Howell had to balance all the factors in keeping us as somewhat of a unit.

We listened to the BBC and Voice of America, but the news was always negative.

I appreciated your notes about Peter and the success of Matthew's surgery, but it disturbs me to learn how life goes on without me. How unnecessary I am! Forgive me. I'm just feeling sorry for myself.

I keep trying to get the money from my job sent to you. Frustration abounds in my not knowing if it's working, no certainty whether I could have any positive effect.

We were all eating tuna almost every day now. I experimented in order to learn the best tuna condiment. Mustard just didn't do it. Ketchup was okay, but by far the best was barbecue sauce, which brought out just the perfect tuna flavor. And it wore well as an everyday diet. Some of the men lost considerable weight— not me.

We hoped for a UN resolution invoking military action. I didn't know if we could be extracted in time for the incoming US troops. Although the Iraqis did not threaten us at all to this point, I didn't think their honor could be trusted. And who knows how much control the officers have over their men? After all, they had

FAITH IN CRISIS

seen us lounging around the pool eating all we want, watching movies. How much of that could they take when they weren't even being fed every day?

October 1

I didn't get a message from you yesterday—the third day in a row without one. I got so paranoid. I have an uncomfortable feeling the pit of my stomach that just doesn't go away.... There is a sense something will happen here in the next couple of weeks. The ambassador believes Bush will do something soon, but I don't think he knows.

I realize we could use the events here as some kind of badge of spirituality. I don't deserve to wear it ... especially since I see myself trapped by my own pride.

Folks will get the idea being a hostage is some sort of laudable state ... an absurdity. A hero is not someone who got trapped.

By the way, I'm upset about the notebooks you write to God. I know you've done it for forever, and for a long time I never gave it much thought. I respected your privacy ... I'm sure you remember the time you caught me looking at one your notebooks. You had left the notebook open on the counter, and I just began reading it. I don't recall what I read. You got mad, and I backed off. I didn't pursue it then. I know it bothers me and we should talk about it.... Maybe I'm jealous of God. Do you really not want me to look at your journals? The one I'm writing is for you.

As the last note to her indicated, my mind wandered to all sorts of oddities. I thought of every little event Shirley and I had experienced together. And I was jealous of what she might experience without me. Crazy, confused thoughts.

October 2

Saddam released some French hostages. Perhaps this was to repair the damage done to the French embassy and delegation.

JIM AND SHIRLEY CARROLL

October 3

I couldn't imagine this closing out before six months. The tension was high. The Kuwaiti resistance had been quiet recently. They'd probably been killed, or perhaps they'd backed off because their actions made thing worse for their families and the other Kuwaitis.

Maurice was stubbornly optimistic. He expressed his thoughts that the Iraqis were going to pull out. But they had 400,000 men in Kuwait—not a strong sign of a pullout.

October 4

The days passed so slowly. We saw a number of fires in the city. I couldn't tell if it was merely garbage being burned or whether the Iraqis were beginning to burn the city. More likely it was the former, because refuse was beginning to accumulate in the absence of regular trash pickup. We were burning our own garbage, making certain the ill-smelling smoke drifted toward the Iraqis.

More and more people were leaving Kuwait. Indians were mostly gone. Philippine citizens were slowly departing. The Iraqis were allowing them to depart because of their nationalities. Once they got out of the city, it was just a short distance to the border, unless they got hung up in the desert. We also suspected Kuwaitis were getting out as they had the chance. I hoped Suhair had gotten out with her children. A few Jordanians were still around the community. We heard they were speculating on property, taking advantage of their new political position, but definitely an uncertain venture, particularly considering the unreliable currency and the absence of a certain Iraqi victory.

October 5

Hot and humid, even into October—typical weather in Kuwait. The trees would be changing colors in the north Georgia mountains, and the deer season approached the rut. Would I see the red and orange leaves again?

Fires still burned in the community, and last night eight to ten explosions blasted out in the neighborhoods. Who knows what the Iraqis were doing? Perhaps the resistance was still active, but our information was limited and of dubious accuracy.

###

October 6

There was such a variety of views in the embassy as to what would happen. Maurice was supremely, and in my view, ridiculously optimistic. Was this just for my benefit? If so, thanks to you, Maurice. Others thought we didn't have much of a chance, but the fact is we didn't know then. Maurice continued to appear well. He was so optimistic and I depended on him for a good word. But I suspected he was not doing as well as he appeared at that point. He said he felt the uncertainty was getting to him. No surprise.

Chapter 13

Bombing Is the Best News

Then there was the uplifting event occurring right in our neighbors' nest. The resistance set off a car bomb in the front doorway of the International Hotel. The series of blasts was wonderfully loud and exciting. The first blast seemed to be from a car in the overhang at the hotel entry area. As best we could determine, a fire was ignited by the first blast, which spread to other cars resulting in a series of gas tank explosions one after another. Barbara climbed up to see over the wall, which put her in the potential line of fire of the explosions.

"Barbara, you've got to get down from there. You'll be hit!" I called to her.

I didn't want to have to dream up a way to care for a blast injury. But of course she didn't mind my call. I suppose she thought it was her duty to learn what was happening. The entire episode required only a few minutes, but the exhilaration provided persisted for several days. We later heard a group from the Kuwaiti resistance had achieved the disruption. Although the higher level officers had been missed, two Iraqi soldiers were killed.

The bombing demonstrated the Iraqis were vulnerable. We all took the event as an uplifting experience, an indication that the Iraqis didn't have full control, a sign that anything could transpire. If they could hit the major billet for the Iraqi officers, then perhaps there was hope for the whole Iraqi system to melt away. But this was only the hope of one trapped.

October 7

No result we knew of followed the hotel bombing, and the Iraqis continued their occupation of the site. More depressed. I struggled to eat and keep my weight up, even though it was a chore. Eating was the one physically constructive thing I could do for myself. And despite the successful hotel bombing, there was still recurring evidence the Iraqis were still taking Americans as hostages.

I got your note about Peter and John going fishing. I'm glad John is taking up his responsibility. I hope John can continue at Covenant College next semester.

I hoped my job was still open in Augusta. If not, then I'd have to call Oklahoma about their offer. I had far too much time to think. What if this happened, then what? What if such and such occurred? Could we walk away from our calling in the Middle East? But I really wasn't thinking straight.

FAITH IN CRISIS

October 8

I composed a letter to be sent by Hameed, who was hoping to get out. His status as an Arab American was supposed to bring him forgiveness from Saddam. He didn't get out, at least not yet.

The content of the letter that never arrived: *First, some business matters.... The most important is my salary here. You should file for payment by sending a typed invoice to NEA/EX/DIR, Department of State, Washington, DC 20520. The invoice should bill for my physician services rendered 16 August–30 Sep 1990 on contract S-445-FA-200. Request payment of $4320 for 240 hours at $18 per hour to be made to us. You should designate an account for the check to be sent to.... Go ahead and send an invoice to them at the end of every month for the amount of $2880 ($18 per hour x 160 hours).*

The next issue is the money from the Kuwait embassy in Washington, DC. I know some families of hostages are getting money from them. You might want to contact Abdullatif to see if he can help. If you have the number of Cathy Abouna, I'm sure they'll know how to contact Louise and Abdullatif. Maybe Kuwait University would even continue to pay my salary.

Let me assure you I'll accept without question any decision you make—selling the house, using the Merrill-Lynch stocks and bonds for cash, borrowing from Dad, anything....

I hope John is able to go back to Covenant next semester. I would not object to a loan.... He may have to support the family if I don't get back ... I want John to go to Urbana for the mission conference if at all possible.

With all the practical worries, I still know that God will take care of you and the children. I have full confidence in that. It won't be easy, but I know His Word is true.

I apologize for repeatedly asking about the information from Dr. Green.... There is no sign of a medical evacuation yet, and even if there is, I might not be counted as one who is eligible to be evacuated.... The grounds which might get me out are that my retinal problem represents an impending detachment, which would result in blindness.

I don't know if I can express to you in a brief letter all I am experiencing here. The physical discomforts are minor compared to the mental anguish. I am now pretty well accustomed to living without air-conditioning.... The food is very bad, you know I'm a picky eater anyway, but I am eating and not losing weight ... but the mental stress is unbelievable ... and it's self-inflicted.

I can't imagine what you're experiencing, but it must be awful, too. Much of the time I have a terrible feeling in the pit of my stomach....

There is still periodic fighting around the embassy compound with gunfire and explosions. This is unnerving, but I don't think we are currently at much physical risk.... All of us are fighting despair and depression one way or another. I awaken very early each morning and just lie there and worry. Every day is the same.

I am totally dependent on the Lord. There isn't any other choice. I know this is for our good, but it is difficult to see the end—it's not possible for me now to know God's plan. But I trust His plan is best for us all ... I welcome His conclusion.

I know I'll need to go back to work as soon as possible, but I'm not sure I'll be mentally able. Maurice says we all may need counseling for depression when we get out.... Please do whatever is necessary to keep yourself mentally okay for the kids....

I pray for you and all the children: John, Peter, Ruth, Rebecca, Timothy, Matthew, and Lydia—that you will all walk by God's Spirit and grace.

Though we are separated physically, I feel we have been one in this event. I pray you feel the same. Let us now be one in the Spirit and soon physically as well. I love you so much.

How long will this last only God knows. I hope this time has great meaning for us. All on the compound want our detention to exist for some purpose.

Please tell Dad and Sally I love them. Comfort them for me.

There were no more resistance attacks on the hotel.

Chapter 14

Shirley's Bubble

Shirley

Our friends, mainly the Christians, had been frank with me.

"Shirley, you've got to tell the children the truth. Their father is surrounded by hundreds of thousands of enemy troops, and the US has to attack. Jim's right in the middle of where the battle will occur. Whatever you've been told, or whatever you think, there's no way to get him out."

I'd heard variations on the same theme for two months—some blunt, some gentle, but all with the same message.

But the most painful were the words directed at me.

"Shirley, you're just ignoring the truth. You're making believe with yourself. You have to plan for the future without Jim."

I knew they had my interest in mind, and they thought I was crazy. And as Christian friends, they had to say what they believed to be the truth. But I couldn't stand it, and I stopped listening.

JIM AND SHIRLEY CARROLL

God put a bubble around me. The Spirit told me Jimmy was going to get out of Kuwait. He was going to be okay. The peace of the Spirit's leading kept me sane and allowed me to protect the children from any imposed fear that their father wouldn't return. "Walk by faith" had been our motto the day the ordeal began, and now faith became an iron-hard entity. There was no earthly reason for this blessing from God. It just arrived, stayed, and shielded.

We therefore made the decision to continue with the life in front of us. After all, that's what walking by faith means. The Scripture messages I got from Jimmy confirmed the plan, and we charged on just like normal because the Lord's protection was normal, no change.

We couldn't linger as if we were waiting for the future, because decisions had to be made. Matthew's birthmarks were in need of another surgery, so I scheduled the procedure. "You're doing what? You're having an elective surgical procedure on one of your children, and Jim's not even around?"

"Yes, that's what we're doing."

In the midst of the surgery plan, Lydia, Timothy, and Matthew managed to make it through a four-week period of chickenpox. I think God sent the itching, scratching, and pink lotion to keep our minds directed straight at the present. The chicken pox blessing.

Camilla, one of my good friends from St. Louis, came down with her daughter. We had known them from our years there in the city. "Shirley, you can't just live day by day like this and expect things to turn out. You need to make a plan and tell the children the truth. You have to be ready to face the fact that maybe Jimmy will never come home." But I had a peace that God would work things out in his timing. What else could we do but live day by day? We continued to pray and kept busy with homeschool.

No money ever materialized from the US State Department or Kuwaiti government in exile. But God's provisions for us were endless, and we never needed for anything. Jimmy's former boss at

FAITH IN CRISIS

the medical school, Tom Swift, started a fund to help support us. The neighbors set up a similar fund, and the donations rolled in. We stopped keeping track. I was still no good at accepting monetary gifts, so ten-year-old Ruth continued to write the thank-you notes.

Huge grocery bags arrived whenever we were hungry. I had never bought Frosted Flakes, so the kids went crazy when they appeared. That was embarrassing. MacDonald's sent us cards for meals. The local service stations give us weekly free cards for gasoline. Our household bills were held in abeyance awaiting Jim's return. Covenant College allowed John to attend with no tuition payments. All these items appeared as gifts from the Lord, and I was further assured of a good ending. The bubble never popped.

Jim and I continued to send messages Bible verses back and forth, subject to the overwhelmed resources of the State Department. One of the Bible passages I sent was I John 4:15–21: "Whoever confesses that Jesus is the son of God, God abides in him ... God is love, and whoever abides in love abides in God .... By this is love perfected with us, so that we may have confidence for the day of judgment.... There is no fear in love, but perfect love casts out fear.... We love, because he first loved us. If someone says, I love God, and hates his brother, he is a liar.... And this commandment we had from him: whoever loves God must also love his brother."

The Lord helped me dispense with fear, because we knew he loved us. Our final confidence was in the day of judgment, but God told me judgment was later, not yet. And another miracle visited. The love I had for my brothers and sisters persisted even when they said to give up on Jim.

With this verse I had written to Jim, "We love you so much and we all continue to pray for you and know that we will be together soon."

Another message I had sent Jim in October was, "We are praying for you. It is difficult for us, too. But our faith is in the

JIM AND SHIRLEY CARROLL

Lord and your return. And we agree with 1 Corinthians 1:9, "God is faithful, by whom you were called into the fellowship of his Son, Jesus Christ our Lord."

###

I had forgotten how beautiful our neighborhood in Augusta was in the fall. God's beauty surrounded us even when Jimmy was trapped in the embassy. We spent time outside, where we could see God's glory. The kids loved playing ball and being out in the yard with its flowers and huge trees. The children were happy and in good spirits, much to the distress of the people who came to visit us. "You all don't even seem upset. I don't get it. Shirley, it just doesn't seem right." The fact that the children remained happy and oblivious to what was deemed a disaster by others actually upset visitors. They didn't share the bubble effect.

###

One of the elders from our church, Phil Hedges, took the job of visiting every week. Phil was a small, slender man with a kind and reassuring manner, and not much hair. There was never an ounce of judgmental attitude in him. There was no criticism from Phil about my handling of the crisis.

Phil worked in Augusta at a business called the Merryland Brick Yard, where clay was excavated and converted into bricks. The children had never seen the operation, and Phil took them on a field trip. Who would have ever thought making bricks could be so interesting to children, but Phil had that easy, gentle manner that was so comforting to the kids.

From the Augusta food bank we got cornflakes, sugar, and flour. I learned to make muffins again, a skill acquired in childhood from my grandmother.

FAITH IN CRISIS

The children loved Phil and looked forward to his visits. He came for lunch and was willing to eat whatever we had, which was not much by usual standards, but enough for us. Phil sat to eat the muffins with us, and we had a party each week. I began to wonder what the neighbors thought about a man's car parked outside our house regularly each week. That's how faithful Phil was.

Chapter 15

More Evacuations; I'm Still Stuck

October 9

On guard duty in the morning at 6:30. Thank the Lord He had supplied a reason to get up out of bed, even if it was just guard duty. I sweltered in the guard post with the door closed, and outside the door the flies were bad. Was there any hope for this to be over? I was really feeling low. I know the Scriptures teach that suffering produces good things—maturity, even joy, but I think I got enough of the message.

And the Romans 8:28 verse kept coming back. I accepted its truth as fact, but I couldn't figure out how it applied. I knew God had the whole thing in hand, but I couldn't figure out how my situation worked for His purpose. A wife and seven children waited for me. How could my not making it back fulfill God's purpose for me? Would I have an answer in this life to the puzzle?

JIM AND SHIRLEY CARROLL

###

October 11

We were privileged to assist with the evacuation of female Kuwaitis and their children who had been born in the US and were therefore US citizens. If we couldn't get ourselves out, at least we could help these moms and their children. Our job was to take information over the phone if they wanted to go, and then transmit the data to Gale Rogers and Barbara Bodine as they scheduled the flights.

The very last of about twelve evacuation flights finally departed. I still felt bad about my mistake with one of the phone numbers. One of the phone numbers I submitted was wrong, and there was no way to contact the family who wanted out. Barbara was furious, rightfully so. I had taken the family's number down incorrectly, and there was no way to fix the mistake. I could only hope they didn't suffer from my error. Even if the family had given the wrong number, it had been my responsibility to keep repeating the number back to them and make sure it was correct. My potential excuse was the transcription of Arabic numbers to English, but I spoke enough Arabic to know the numbers, so no real excuse.

We're told there wouldn't be any other planes leaving Kuwait. The Iraqis weren't going to supply any more for departures of those who might be allowed to leave. There wouldn't be any need for another unless the Western men were released. All this meant any opportunity to get out of Kuwait was finished. The Western hostages, including us on the compound, were stuck until the conclusion, whatever that might be.

The shooting and explosions were reduced. Iraqi control was consolidated.

FAITH IN CRISIS

Westerners were still being picked up throughout the city after a lull of seven to ten days. My regular caller in the community was late in phoning in. He called every morning when I was on guard duty answering the phone. I was concerned he might have been taken. How peculiar it was in the guard post—kicking back and trying to relax, answering the phone like a small business proprietor.

My friend Hameed, who was supposed to get out and carry the letter I wrote, was held up again by the Iraqis, and he didn't get his release from the compound. Both the letter and the tape I dictated for Shirley never got there. Considering the way I sounded on the tape, it was probably for the best.

October 12

What would transpire when we leave here? Will it be to Iraq, the US, or will we just be taken out horizontally?

There was much to be thankful for. Several on the compound had turned to the Lord. Who knows if these were "foxhole" conversions? God knows.

October 13

Yesterday one of the newscasters said military force would not be used for at least two months. Roman 8:28 kept coming back to me. I devoured the verse. I never doubted its veracity. I just couldn't figure out how the verse fit in my situation. But I also knew it didn't matter if I could figure it out or not.

October 14

We were still continuing fuel consumption at a specific rate, which limited the amount of time we could communicate. We got so angry with the peace groups suggesting continuation of the

JIM AND SHIRLEY CARROLL

sanctions for another six months or a year. What did they think would happen to the innocents during the sanctions? I suppose the question was whether I was willing to give up a period of my life to save the lives of others who would otherwise die in a war. I think the answer was yes, if there was a clear rationale. But I didn't see the basis clearly.

Chapter 16

The Well

October 15

Paul Brown, "Brownie," had been digging in the garden area for some time. Most of us thought the exercise was pointless, driven by his own frustration. But we understood and accepted his need to dig. All of us were digging in one way or another, and we all had excavations of some type to pursue. How could you hope for water in the desert? But Paul seemed to know there should be water. He had worked in grounds keeping for years and knew secrets.

We watched Paul digging by himself day after day. We let him alone in his personal, self-inflicted misery. But after some time he struck water, and its flow was strong and filled the hole even as uses were found for the water. More diggers joined the effort. The source of the water was uncertain: perhaps a spring, some type of runoff from the sea, or maybe drainage water stored in a cavern from previous years watering the embassy garden.

We had no way to be sure about the purity of the water. We couldn't drink it. But it had all kinds of uses for us. We could use it for showers, for keeping the pool full, and most important for watering a garden. Ample seeds were discovered in the embassy stores. We could even taunt the Iraqis watching down on us from the hotel by washing our cars. They had shut off our water, but here we were luxuriating in our excess. But the big push was the garden—fresh vegetables when there were likely none in the rest of Kuwait.

October 16

Bush said we're in it "for the long haul." Easy for him to say. But the water increased the possibility of our making the "long haul."

October 17

Still no way out in sight. We used more and more of our supplies of food, water, and the all-important fuel used to run the generator for State Department communication. If the fuel ran out, would we be forced to give up and surrender ourselves to the Iraqis? Was it possible for us to get out through Baghdad because of our conferred diplomatic status? Probably not, and no men have done so yet. The most likely scenario was that we'd end up in Baghdad awaiting the end of the whole thing.

October 18

We were worried the US would decide not to go to war and seek a negotiated settlement. Such an agreement could leave us stuck for an indefinite period.

###

Last night we watched pornographic movies. Wednesday was the standard day for these films, and there was an ample supply of them in the Marine barracks. The movies made me feel worse about missing you, but I couldn't help watching. The women usually absented themselves on Wednesday evening.

October 19

I am afraid Matthew, Timmy, and Lydia wouldn't know me. I don't know how you were managing financially. I was assured God was taking care of you. I prayed for you that you would walk by the Spirit.

October 20

I got the message that two men in the church were praying for John's tuition.

I still had trouble conceiving this was all really happening. Perhaps I would awaken tomorrow morning from the dream.

Chapter 17

The Pullback That Never Happened

There were rumors in the community that the Iraqis might pull back. These seemed to come from several sources, so we hoped there might be some validity to them. Already there seemed to be troop movements, but they rotated the soldiers often anyway, and we had no cogent expectation of their all heading north and out of Kuwait. Of course, everyone hung hopes on a pleasant rumor, and I was afraid it was mostly that only. Why would they want to give up territory won in battle without another fight? We should know in a few days what the story would be on this. I counted the room lights at the International Hotel every night, and the number of rooms occupied had not changed appreciably. How much we look at little details that probably mean nothing.

JIM AND SHIRLEY CARROLL

October 21

There was no further indication of an Iraqi pullback, no sign of their leaving the hotel next door. The number of room lights didn't vary.

I'm worn down this morning with a sense of sin—both my own and that of the world. What a mess we made. The inhumanity and cruelty that I've seen here in Kuwait has become routine to me. Although the Iraqis are the main source of it now, you know the Kuwaitis did their share. But my own sin is foremost. I absolutely cannot be content with the present situation. And we are told to be content in all things. I am so resentful. I pray to God to release me from the contentious spirit. I am useless to myself in the current state of mind ... I still suffer from this idea it was my pride which got us into this, that I could do some great thing in the Middle East.... I pray for the opportunity to exchange experiences with you over this thing in the deepest, spiritual sense.

October 22

The twenty-third was the day something was supposed to happen. Why had they chosen the twenty-third? The twenty-third Psalm perhaps. Maurice remained in contact with the NECK, and the elders still present in Kuwait had informed him the church was praying for some kind of resolution on that date. All theology aside, I was thankful for their specific prayer. And then, seemingly independently, a number of rumors cropped up around that date. I tried not to get caught up in the possibility. From my vantage point there was little to confirm the rumors. The number of lights in the hotel was the same again last night. Troop movements around us were basically the same.

###

FAITH IN CRISIS

October 23

This was the supposed day for an Iraqi pullback, and nothing changed. Last night an Iraqi patrol car drove around making an announcement, but I couldn't understand the words. Even our Arabic speakers couldn't decipher their message.

In the news were reports of various kinds of releases, but they seemed to be exaggerated. What was not reported were the continuing sweeps by the Iraqis to get more hostages. I wondered if these were reported in the US news, of if they were hidden by the State Department. The Iraqis continued to loot the city.

October 24

Nothing happened due to the prayers of the church, as far as I know, nothing from my vantage point. We heard hostages have been released—fourteen Americans, thirty British, and all the French—about 350 in total. Saddam was trying to lighten the tension. Why them and not us?

I just never know what His will is for a specific event. I do believe it's within God's will for me to return. I just don't know when. I know He'll give us all we need.

###

October 25

The well dug under the supervision of Paul Brown was a Godsend. We got water from it for showers. The water was piped up to the roof tank over the swimming pool shower area where it was heated by the afternoon sun. By later in the afternoon we had warm showers, a real blessing. The showers were, we hoped, a preview of freedom. The water was also useful for taunting the Iraqis. Several times we used the water to wash the cars in the compound, a real insult for them after they went to so much trouble turning off our city water. We didn't use the water for drinking because we had no way of testing its bacterial content. Also, the water was brackish with a high salt content. But the water was also used for a garden, where it was a real advantage for us. And finding a water well in the desert was a message from God.

The well inspired us all. I ran every day making circles around the compound—maybe two miles a day. I was sure the exercise helped. And we still had the pool open due to the well. With the cooler nights, however, the water was a bit too cold for me.

And I continued to stuff down the tuna to maintain my weight.

October 26

I managed to get a letter out through the French being released. At least that was my understanding. I had no idea how the letter was given to the one who transported it. It was possible, given the declining level of fuel, that our ability to exchange messages could stop.

As I was on guard duty in the morning from six to nine, I received a call about 7:30 inquiring whether the embassy knew the whereabouts of "Jim Carlow or Jim Carl." I told the caller I thought he was referring to me. The caller said a "highly placed" Kuwaiti was looking for me. I got the impression the caller had connections to the emir, probably my wishful thinking. The caller had all the information about our kids. I asked if there was any way to get money to Shirley. I was hopeful. The caller sounded sincere and the timing, with me on guard duty, was providential. I didn't know if the call had any effect. Maybe the whole thing was some kind of Iraqi trick to find me. No more information came from the caller.

October 27

The early morning just after I awakened was the worst time. The reality of the situation closed in on me. I see two armies of half a million facing each other. It could be the largest single battle in history.

The news from the Saudis said that Saddam was fortifying his southern position, "digging in" and building a "wall." Also, the Iraqis were also reported to be building a "wall" near Mutla ridge to the north of the city. The word I heard for the first time was "berm." Could a berm impede a modern army?

Chapter 18

Halloween, Pigeon Meat, God Only Wise, and Kurt Vonnegut

We couldn't stay forever. As far as food and water go, we could make it at least for another two or three months. But the diesel fuel used for communication was a bigger concern. I didn't think the State Department would let the embassy stay open without communication ability. The thinking was we wouldn't be safe without ability to communicate with the US. When the allies' attack came, they would have no way to notify us about taking cover, or about any potential action by the Iraqis. And if the embassy had to close, we would have to give up to the Iraqis. None of us wanted to go to Baghdad.

October 28

I felt extremely impatient in the morning. *Thanks for your message about Tom Swift's call. It's good to know I'll have a job if this is over in a reasonable amount of time.... I still have the daydream of getting back to our work in Kuwait ... but the difficulties are overwhelming ... there won't be any satisfactory school or other conditions in Kuwait for the kids for several years... the threat of military action won't disappear after this is over.... I ask myself periodically if this were over now, could I still be thankful for this? The answer is still yes. I don't know how much more of that response I have left in me. God knows, though.*

October 29

We were closer to the edge without falling over it. Diplomatic measures failed. Yevgeny Primakov, Gorbachev's special emissary to Iraq, had gone to Baghdad with his immediate impetus for the trip being the concern about Soviet citizens trapped in Iraq. Just prior to Primakov's mission, Russian newspapers ran letters from worried parents complaining that their sons were not being allowed out of Iraq. Deputies in the Soviet and Russian parliaments received similar letters from constituents asking why the government was not acting to protect its citizens. The day before Primakov left Iraq, a government spokesman acknowledged that thousands of Soviets wishing to depart from Iraq were being denied exit visas. Last week's meeting between President Bush and Primakov had generated much speculation about a possible Soviet diplomatic initiative to end the Gulf crisis. But expectations were inflated.

Primakov provided Bush a firsthand account of his discussions in Baghdad with Iraqi President Saddam Hussein and floated some ideas for a political solution. Primakov, however, seemed to back the US in whatever course of action it pursued. President Bush rejected any proposals for a settlement that would reward

FAITH IN CRISIS

Iraq for its aggression. Thus, the Primakov initiative failed, leaving few other choices. War remained in front of us.

By all reports locally there were fewer troops and equipment in the city, but we didn't know if they went north or south. The Iraqis readied for the onslaught from the US-led coalition. Still we were in the way.

October 30

Confirming the approaching conflict, the UN resolution passed yesterday dealing with reparations, war crimes, and embassy resupply. There was no turning back from war. Perhaps the "resupply" would be important for us here. The fantasy was still that helicopters would come in over the wall for rescue, or that the copters would arrive for the resupply and we could leave on the "resupply" copters.

The ambassador has told the State Department that our limit for communication abilities was November 20. We could probably get by for a while longer, but the end of that communication was in sight. The choices were: give up and go to Baghdad, resupply by some means, stay without communication ability, or start the allies' attack against the Iraqis. These choices were in no way in our hands. The State Department and the president would make these decisions. Also, the generator was suffering from overuse. It could go out anytime. So far the least dramatic solution has always been the one to develop. Most likely they'll stretch out the communication by decreasing the length and frequency of the calls.

Bush noted the "plight" of the embassy in his news conference. Was this some kind of diplomatic signal that he might act on our dilemma? We're going to have to decrease our communication time. Failure of the generator would force a quicker decision by our friends in Washington: give up or stay without communication.

JIM AND SHIRLEY CARROLL

Our water supply had about three months remaining. Our food supply was about the same, though the quality and variety would get worse. We could last until the end of January, longer with achievable rationing. Would six months be enough for the sanctions to work?

Then there was suddenly much more troop activity immediately around the embassy.

I pray the children are doing well in school. I pray Matthew is healing well. I'm anxious to see how the surgery looks.

October 31

We had a Halloween party. We were supposed to dress up as someone famous. *You know how I feel about that kind of thing, even under the best of circumstances, but I'm trying to think of something. I don't want to hurt morale by being negative.*

November 1

I didn't dress up in a costume for the Halloween party last night—I don't change my ways very well.

November 2

Bush seems to be referring now to the embassy here. I hope that means something is planned. Our communication abilities can last only a few more weeks—even if the generator holds together.

I just learned that we may be able to go for a while longer on battery power for communication after the gasoline runs out, so our life span here might be lengthened.

I haven't heard from you regularly—only once in the last five days.

November 3

I appreciated Shirley's quotation from Jeremiah 33:5 about restoration. *"They are coming in to fight against the Chaldeans and to fill them with the dead bodies of men whom I shall strike down in my anger and my wrath."* I knew whom Shirley meant by the Chaldeans. The Chaldees were just north of us in present day Iraq. They shouldn't mess with my Shirley.

November 4

I got a letter out via a Merrill-Lynch employee who was departing. I asked Shirley to call Senator Nunn to express concern about the sanctions not working. Our ability to send messages was likely not to last much longer. I was sending messages just about every day. I received three or four a week from her. We tried to set up a method for letters, but it didn't seem plausible.

We still had plenty to eat, though it was not appetizing. My weight was holding at about 65 kilograms.

###

We tried to catch pigeons for meat, which would be a tasty addition to our diet. Three of us set up the trap in the open field that used to be the parking lot for the residents' cars. The trap was a wire container about two feet in all three dimensions with one side open, used for transporting containers of various kinds, perhaps milk. We baited the trap with any kind of leftover food particles we could find. The pigeons were probably desperate, too. The trap was then tilted up at an angle, and a stick tied to a cord was used to prop up the trap. We stretched out the cord about fifty feet and knelt down behind some large tanks and waited. Sure enough the pigeons arrived. They had not yet fled the city. We actually trapped several and then began to consider how we would keep them and how many we would need for dinner. Trapping the creatures was not going to be a problem. Our unexpected success brought renewed interest in the project, but the State Department did not approve. Apparently the ambassador had not thought our success was likely, but now that we had prospered, the prospect of cleaning, preparing and eating the creatures was imminent.

The State Department vetoed the meal. Their experts felt the risk of pigeon-borne diseases was too likely. As far as I knew, there was no histoplasmosis or coccidiodomycosis in Kuwait. I had seen zero cases during my several-year medical experiences in the country. But I supposed they were just being cautious with our health. The chief risk would likely have been during the cleaning process. Thus, the pigeons with their fat breasts were freed. But we wanted meat. Never in my life had I been without meat for so long (except, of course, for the tuna, which no longer counted as meat on my scale).

The weather had cooled and we were more comfortable, but I had no warm clothes for colder weather. I rummaged through the Marine barracks and located two sweaters that the Marines had left behind. They were now my sweaters. If I returned home, the sweaters would accompany me.

###

We remained bereft of sufficient responsibilities. I had guard duty three hours a day, read the Bible, and played the piano in the residence. I'm sure those who were near the residence grew tired of my playing the same hymn over and over on the grand piano. My choice was "Immortal, Invisible God Only Wise" by Walter C. Smith. The first verse:

FAITH IN CRISIS

Immortal, invisible, God only wise,
In light inaccessible hid from our eyes,
Most blessèd, most glorious, the Ancient of Days,
Almighty, victorious, Thy great Name we praise.

I loved the hymn, but my choice of it was based mainly on the fact it was easy to play.

I worked a little in the office writing my personal journal to Shirley and jogged for about thirty minutes, but the days were never filled.

November 5

We continued to burn fuel at the same rate, which would lead to our being out by the end of November. The food was usually some variation on tuna and rice. The ambassador was pushing the development of the garden. We got mixed signals about our ability to stay in the compound. The physical conditions really didn't matter much anymore. The lack of preferred food, the absence of ice, the lack of adequate cleaning facilities, and the lack of electricity didn't make much difference.

###

The electric guys figured out how to charge car batteries for reading lights. These were a great help in passing the nights after the movie was over. The reading times late into the night allowed escape that approached reality, and I was by this time able to concentrate. I read books I'd never otherwise read, *A Bright and Shining Lie* by John Paul Vann, a great treatise about our failures in Vietnam, the Gore Vidal biographies of Lincoln and Aaron Burr, and all the Kurt Vonnegut novels I could find. All these were consumed late into the night by the light produced with a small glove compartment bulb powered by a car battery removed from a vehicle.

> JIM AND SHIRLEY CARROLL

###

Lena and Gerald and their two children were having terrible problems. They were still living in the university apartments in Shuwaikh. I was certain they had trouble getting food. Someone must have brought food in for them. I was grateful for their occasional calls.

November 6

I read Bible passages on patience, but they don't "take." I'm rebellious against God's dealing with me. It's also clear he is not finished and that I have far to go. But why should you and the children be dragged into this? Lord, I see your will, but I'm not sure I like it.

November 7

My journal was an escape from all we were facing. I could complain with intimate freedom. *Every day is a new nightmare. I don't think it will ever be over.... As much as the atrocities and aggressions that have occurred, it is still questionable whether it is worth fighting over. Should there be a war over little Kuwait, a war that might kill thousands of US soldiers...? So we are left with no exit ... I just can't stand it ... I don't see how God can separate me from my children. Yet I know God handles me no differently than he has others in the past. Other men better men than me have been taken from their children. I have no right to question his wisdom. Everything flows from it. His mercies are everlasting. But I can't see the reason for this great pain ... I love you.*

November 8

I appreciated your quote from Jeremiah 39:18, "For I will surely save you, and you shall not fall by the sword, but you have your life as a prize of war, because you have put your trust in me, declares the Lord." Thanks to the Lord for the answer to my jeremiad.

FAITH IN CRISIS

The news was once again inflammatory, and everyone's hopes rose that something was going to happen. We thought Saddam delighted in all the attention. World leaders came to his door begging for hostages. The focus of attention was the most important thing to him. Surely he must know he can't win a real war against the US and Britain.

Chapter 19

War Preparations

Apparently the Iraqis expected an attack from the sea. They dug their tanks in along the beach with their gun turrets pointed offshore. How could we survive if the US returned fire in our direction? The US artillery would require perfect accuracy to keep us safe.

I tried to learn to tell the difference between a T-55 tank and a T-72 tank, but I never got it. Even in the pictures in the *Jane's* book looked identical to me. We watched the Iraqis moving the tanks around, sometimes digging them into semi-concealed positions near the beach and then moving them again without apparent purpose. Then there were the BMP-1 infantry-fighting vehicles and the MT-LB armored personnel carriers, identified by *Jane* magazine photographs. The Iraqis maintained several other weapons along the beach across the road from the embassy. Type 63 107 mm MRL (Multiple Rocket Launcher) batteries were posted on the other side of Gulf Road. All the Iraqi defenses were directed toward the sea.

JIM AND SHIRLEY CARROLL

We had been preparing for war on the compound for several weeks with emergency medical supplies, food, and water stored in the basement of the chancery. The act of preparation for disaster resulted in the others looking more worried. I was grateful for that. I was not afraid of the possibility of the coming battle, and I relished the prospect.

One of the first tasks to provide our bunker entailed filling sandbags with dirt and sand. Then we piled the bags around the windows of the chancery basement and plugged the holes with plastic. We might have been able to keep out some of the poison gas if it was used against us.

The State Department continually wanted a report of our supply status.

I was certain there would be war. I don't know if the ambassador was acting on accurate information or his own opinion, but we were in preparation for something. If there was a battle, we might not fare well here. We were in the middle of the city surrounded by thousands of Iraqi troops. I doubted whether the US forces could get to us before the Iraqis did. We would die here as "heroes."

We thus prepared the compound for war. How odd that these provisions were uplifting. The parking area was slowly opened to serve as a helicopter landing area. Over the course of perhaps five days the cars were gradually moved to the side. Their slow serial removal was accomplished so that the Iraqi officer corps watching down from the International Hotel balconies wouldn't identify the maneuver as a purposeful act. My mind briefly reverted to my first visit to Kuwait when I stayed at the same hotel and looked out from one of the same balconies.

The stanchions of the basketball goals in the same area of the former parking lot were still a potential obstruction for landing craft. In order to avoid the Iraqis' noticing any change, the supports were sawed partially through, leaving enough of the post to

FAITH IN CRISIS

maintain the goal erect but so little still intact that the goal could be pushed over and removed quickly. The area was cleared of even small debris such as stones and sticks, any object that might become a dangerous projectile from the rotating helicopter blades. We could imagine the rhythmic whirring of the blades as the craft appeared over the compound walls and the accompanying sound of the basketball goal crashing to the ground just in time to clear the field.

We speculated on the type of helicopter that would come for us. We agreed the most likely candidate was the Sikorsky UH-60 Black Hawk, an all-purpose attack-and-rescue craft. The only question was the copter's carrying power. How many would be required to evacuate the twenty-eight of us and at the same time still possess sufficient firepower to defend the perimeter? Could the perimeter actually be protected from the surrounding Iraqis?

Preparation of the bunker was more serious as far as I was concerned. It represented a last-ditch survival area for us all. The chancery had a large, below-ground room in the rectangular shape of an auditorium with windows around the sides near the ceiling, just like a basement. The engineers among us said the room required reinforcement to prevent the ground floor of the chancery from collapsing into the basement. They designed a way to shore up the ceiling of the basement with steel reinforcements.

The ceiling was a large, single concrete slab. The choice of the engineers was to create a reinforced column in the center of the room. Four large safes were, with great difficulty, hauled down to the basement in the center of the room. These were welded together to form a structural base for the ceiling. Power for the enclosure was run from the small generator to the bunker. The underground stairwell was reinforced to prevent its blockage. The bunker was stocked with food supplies, water, flak jackets, chemical toilets, and stretchers.

JIM AND SHIRLEY CARROLL

A sound system was installed to serve two purposes. The first, of course, was entertainment. The more serious purpose was to provide sound cover, perhaps *Flight of the Valkyries*, for a helicopter rescue when the time came.

The fix-it folks in the group were quite able to manage all parts of the construction. The sandbags around the windows blocked any light from entering. The few remaining cracks were once again sealed to prevent gas from coming into the bunker. We all doubted that gas could be stopped completely. There were gas masks available but not enough for everyone. No matter. The arms dealers in the compound told us the masks were inadequate. The supplies were topped off with military Meals Ready to Eat (MREs).

The plan for the coming attack by the allies to rescue Kuwait, presumably communicated to the ambassador by the State Department, was relayed to us by the ambassador. Should we still be in the compound when the war began we would be notified shortly before. The attack of US forces would come at night, and we would all be awakened and informed. We would then proceed quietly to the bunker. Minimal noise and activity were required to prevent the Iraqis from observing the movement. We were told to keep a small bag packed in case we were allowed to bring anything, which seemed unlikely anyway. But the simple act of packing the bag enhanced my mood. As the attack began, carpet-bombing would be laid down around the perimeter of the compound. What a great term, "carpet-bombing," evoking the picture of firepower so dense that nothing could survive within its clutches. Then, when the Iraqis had been cleared out, the helicopters would come in for the rescue.

I didn't know how real the possibility really was. I wondered if the ambassador was doing this on his own or under orders from Washington. Or perhaps it was his way of keeping us occupied and hopeful. If war came we likely wouldn't have much notice, else

FAITH IN CRISIS

the information would seep out through the compound's porous information system. Many of us remained in communication with folks outside, and we wouldn't be able to keep our mouths shut.

What about the other Westerners out in the community? There was no way they would have a similar opportunity. Our advantage was that we were in a known location in a group. And if we were extracted, the others in the community would remain at even greater risk. The Iraqis might choose to take out their frustration on them, or they could even be killed by US carpet-bombing.

We were moving to some point of decision. Our communication fuel, it was said, could run out sometime during the period November 20–28. After that our battery power would last about three weeks. I don't understand how that calculation was made or how the "batteries" will work, and the calculations kept being revised upward. I was thankful there were those here who understood such things. Perhaps the information we were given was purposely incorrect, thinking that monitored conversations with those in the community were a good method of delivering disinformation. I didn't understand why the batteries couldn't be recharged with other sources here, such as the auto engines or the small gasoline generators.

The point of all this worry about communication was central. Our food and water supplies were good for perhaps four more months by my analysis, but if we ran out of communication ability, then what? The ambassador couldn't communicate with the State Department. We wouldn't know if or when there was going to be an attack. If the Iraqis decided to enter the compound, we would have no means of communicating our condition. Finally, would the State Department even allow us to stay here without communication? Would the ambassador accept their will if he were told to abandon the site?

Chapter 20

Binary Weapons, Rania

November 9

The ambassador was going to talk with us today. Maybe there was another announcement or decision in the offing. Bush said we had "two weeks of supplies." I wondered how the ambassador could introduce the news, whatever it was, in a positive manner. Bush indicated the US war effort wouldn't be ready for two to three months.

Maurice was working on arrangements to get himself out because of his clergy status. I was jealous. Of course, I wanted him to get out. For a while I had been dependent on his comfort and optimism, but now that was reduced. He was getting discouraged, too. Who could blame him? Maurice thought he had a way out but there were continual stalls.

I heard my Kuwait University salary might be reinstated. Yeah, sure.

November 10

No new information emerged from the ambassador. Either we had misunderstood or the plan, unknown to us, changed. Everything was taking longer than I ever dreamed.

###

November 11

We heard Secretary of State James Baker's trip resulted in the parties agreeing that war may be necessary. Ramsey Clark, the eternal pacifist, was here in the region saying the US was wrong to consider war.

The ambassador encouraged us. He expressed his strong desire to stay here.

November 12

My thoughts about the coming battle grew exponentially with the passage of time. I imagined the largest battle in history with one million men on the field of conflict. *I believe God is protecting me.*

There was talk of "resupplying" the embassy. And the accompanying dream scenario was that helicopters would come in and take us out. The "resupply" would be a ruse to get the copters in. It all seemed like a fantasy.

###

November 13

We believed the Iraqis were installing poison gas around the embassy. I learned the term "binary weapons" for the first time from those in the embassy more familiar with weapons systems. "Binary" meant the weapon was set up in a nontoxic form with two

FAITH IN CRISIS

components separated from each other in the weapon itself. Only when the two components were mixed was the toxin available to be released, hence the adjective, "binary."

The canisters of chemical agents, or whatever they were, were placed around the quadrants of the embassy and wires were run from the canisters to another location. We presumed the Iraqis were setting up a method of ignition, and the resulting toxic substances would be carried into the embassy by the prevailing breeze. So here was another source of worry, based on a more objective observation than what we had seen so far. If war came and the wind was right, we were done.

Last night at dinner we had a brief discouraging word from Gale. She looked particularly frazzled after the diplomats had completed one of their daily, mysterious meetings, and she ran hands through her mane of curly hair. "We're toast." She invoked the image of bread placed in a toaster. We had to assume the information the diplomats received in their daily meeting was particularly bad. They were privy to news or facts, which were not distributed to us. Gale was usually not so committal, so it must have been bad.

As a testimony of the resounding ambiguity we experienced, Maher called with a request. He was one of the young doctors on our staff at Mubarak, and I had not seen him since much earlier in the summer, long before the invasion. His family was Palestinian, and I was surprised he was still in Kuwait. How did he know I was in the embassy? If he knew, then every Iraqi in Kuwait must know. "Professor, I've been trying to reach you. I'm calling about Rania. She's still in the hospital at Mubarak. No one can find her parents. Professor, you've got to get her out of here."

"There's nothing I can do. I'm trapped here in the embassy."

JIM AND SHIRLEY CARROLL

"Everybody knows you'll get out." How did they know? "When you do, you've got to take Rania with you."

"How can I do that? I can't even get myself out."

"When this is over, when the Iraqis run away, there'll be such confusion that you'll be able to just take her. No one will stop you."

How could I categorize or integrate such a request?

November 14

I got your message about Jimmy and Raj. I would be delighted to have them, but I doubt it'll work. They would require money and visas, and we can't supply those now. But if you can do it, I'm in favor.

Jimmy and Raj were Peter's best friends from Kuwait. They had traveled together the streets of Kuwait with their skateboards. Jimmy was the son of an Indian mother and a Palestinian father. His father, a Druz, was abusive, and Jimmy suffered the worst of it. Raj was the son of Indian parents. His parents were divorced, and his mom lived in Kuwait working at the Kuwait English School and caring for Raj and his sister.

Jimmy and Raj had been in Egypt during the invasion with a mission team from the NECK, and they ended up stranded there with no money and no way to return to Kuwait. The Egyptians wouldn't let them stay. Since they were not Kuwaiti citizens but teenagers without means of support, it was uncertain when or if they would ever be able to return to Kuwait. They were adolescents without a country. Could we take them on? Could Shirley do it by herself? Raj was an easy kid, bright, and probably not too hard to handle. Jimmy, on the other hand, was a real handful, just as bright, but wow.

Was this a good idea? Sure, why not. Shirley had only seven children, no husband in sight, and no money. No problem for God.

FAITH IN CRISIS

Who was this ridiculous amazing woman who saw things with so much greater clarity than I did? I had to get home. I didn't want to let go of all this.

###

It was the middle of the month, and still there was no plan known to me about the communication equipment. We kept hearing Bush's concern about the embassy's supplies. Was this really an issue, or was the talk just talk to keep up the public's interest? We knew the embassy was just a secondary, no a tertiary, matter.

For a change I had guard duty at the front gate during the evening meal, and I was regretting the time away from the group. Joe came out to keep me company. "Hey, Jim, you look lonely out here. I'll eat with you." He had brought up at plate of spaghetti and marinara sauce for me.

"Yup, I could use the company, and the food." We sat down on high stools in front of the bulletproof glass. Just then two sad-looking Iraqi recruits came walking along on their beat. Joe and I moved our plates up where they were visible to the soldiers and made an effort to eat slowly and with relish over the choice dish. We made sustained eye contact with the two kids, staring at them as they walked by. They reciprocated, but we finally won the staring contest. They looked away, and we had secured one small victory over our keepers. The question occurred to me whether the glass was really bulletproof. Later on I mentioned this to one of the diplomats. "Don't count on it."

###

JIM AND SHIRLEY CARROLL

November 15

Our food was becoming more and more boring. The commercial liquor supplies were nearly consumed, replaced by various homebrews. I wasn't busy enough to keep my mind occupied—just guard duty, prayer time, simple meds for various people, exercise, laundry, some piano playing—and the time dragged on. We looked forward to dinner and movies in the evening with drinks. I started having one or two drinks in the evening. It helped me lose concentration.

Last evening I must have had more to drink than I anticipated. I settled down in the lawn chair to watch the movie with the others. I closed my eyes for a moment as I leaned back my head, and I suddenly got dizzy with nausea. I thought I might vomit. I was concerned for me to start throwing up after drinking too much would set a bad example. Plus, for the "doc" to get sick would be bad for morale. I pulled my faculties back together, got up, and walked back to my bed in the medical building. I hoped my walking wasn't too bad. I made it back, flopped on the mattress, and went soundly to sleep.

November 16

I appreciated Shirley's cable about her willingness to come and try to get me out. I didn't know what was best. I didn't want to put her in any danger, but I surely wanted out. I considered it for a long time and reached no conclusion.

November 19

The last two days, I worked on letters to go out with those who were supposed to leave. None have left. I wanted those who are going to get out but I'm jealous, and they can't leave. Maurice was totally focused on his leaving, no more attention to me. The others who may leave have that privilege because of their Arab extraction. Two of the three didn't speak Arabic, and they would find themselves in trouble in Baghdad.

We thought there would be a war resolution soon. But it appears the US won't be ready to fight until February. We decreased the power usage, something we could have done weeks ago. We were relying on the State Department to develop a plan, but they failed to do so. So the power will last until mid-December with battery power for several weeks after that. With a big stretch we might even make it until February.

I continue to believe I'll get through this.

###

November 20

The news was bad this morning. Gorbachev said he wouldn't support the resolution calling for military force. Could this prevent the war resolution? And the news was that a Marine landing exercise failed. How was that possible? Saddam was bringing in another 250,000 troops. We saw many trucks with artillery pieces going south early this morning. *This just keeps building and building without any sustained movement to a conclusion.* And then there were the poison gas canisters around the embassy. *I think there is a serious question whether we'll get out of this alive. I pray you'll be okay with the kids if I don't survive. I would certainly want you to find someone else if it comes to that. This living alone is intolerable. I don't want you to experience it for the rest of your life ... God gives me great confidence in your ability to bear up and continue in the face of adversity.*

JIM AND SHIRLEY CARROLL

November 21

I read through Kings, and I saw people in pain similar to mine. Some brought it on themselves and some did not. I wondered why God allowed this. I know others have asked the same question.

I don't see the end to this. Why would Saddam ever free us?

Chapter 21

Thanksgiving

November 22

Paul Brown dug a miracle well in the compound, yes, a well in the middle of the desert. The resulting garden was productive, and the fresh vegetables were a blessing from the Lord. The green plants, the lettuce, onions, carrots, radishes, erupted out of the sandy soil induced by the well water and temperate fall weather. Hameed cultivated the vegetable miracle, and the water supplied by the desert well was the voucher that purchased the blooms. The cooler weather and bright sunlight in the deepening fall enhanced the growth. We had all the vegetables and more that we could consume for the Thanksgiving meal.

Not all in the compound were enthusiastic about a day of Thanksgiving. "How are we supposed to be thankful when there are 400,000 Iraqis on our tails? Who wants to celebrate our captivity in a war zone?" Not unreasonable questions. But those of us who favored the celebration won out, and we were Thanksgiving dinner-bound.

JIM AND SHIRLEY CARROLL

Indeed we had been blessed in a remarkable manner, even in the midst of all the trouble. We had an abundance of water now, all the fresh vegetables we could eat, rice, spaghetti, an endless supply of condiments, and thousands of cans of tuna imported from Thailand.

We ate the Thanksgiving Day dinner in the formal dining room of the embassy residence around the large dining table with silver candlesticks and the linen tablecloth. We sat for the meal in several shifts to accommodate all twenty-eight of the compound occupants. Our main dish was tuna lasagna accompanied by onion soup, and fresh green salad with vinegar and oil. Some canned food crept into the menu for variety, green beans and pumpkin pie. I ate everything, even the pie. The meal was served on the embassy residence china embossed with the gold seal of the United States, and the silverware was the US finest.

Altogether the meal was a fitting Thanksgiving. A church service followed, and Maurice led with a homily on giving thanks to God. The twenty-third Psalm was on the minds of most. It was hard to avoid. We considered: "You prepare a table before me in the presence of my enemies." (v. 5a) How could we think of anything else with the Iraqi officer corps peering down at us from the hotel above?

The commercial alcohol supply was running low at that point. But the deficiency was made up by homemade wine. The source was the date palms that populated the embassy grounds. I wasn't sure how the men got the dates down from the tops of the palms, but the winemaking skills of expats in a country where alcohol products were not legal served the purpose. Thus, the words of the verse were fulfilled there as well: "my cup overflows." (v. 5c)

The day melted back into the usual routines, but the thoughts of Thanksgiving lingered over several of us. We knew the rest of the Psalm: "Surely goodness and mercy shall follow me all the days of my life, and I shall dwell in the house of the Lord forever."

FAITH IN CRISIS

(v.6) If we had known the Lord's provisions previously, how could we doubt His new work? We saw the Lord provide a well in the desert, fresh vegetables for us when no one else in Kuwait had them, a meal with the best china and silverware, and all the wine we needed. How could we doubt his endowment for the rest of our lives, no matter what that might be?

The day was a blessing without question. But given my weak humanity, my mind slipped back into the same patterns, but perhaps a little better.

November 23

I missed another day of journaling in order to write a letter to send via Maurice. He was impatient to get out, just like the rest of us, but at least he had a bead on the possibility, a free pass as a member of the clergy. Would the remarkable day of Thanksgiving last in my mind?

The days rolled by without any State Department decision known to us about how long we could remain in the embassy. Such things may depend on the UN decision. Bush has told the troops they'll be in the Middle East war zone until it's over.

November 25

I got three messages from Shirley last night, very uplifting. I was thankful to hear Peter was maturing and doing well. Due to my confusing messages to her, she was in a quandary about whether to come and beg Saddam for my release.

The Lord continued to test me. Last night I got a shock when some paperwork I was depending on didn't come through. The paperwork was distributed ceremoniously, and every other name but mine was called. The State Department was to supply official correspondence for each of us that might serve to get us through the Iraqi Baghdad network, if it came to that. But it didn't come through for me as yet. Frankly it probably wouldn't make much difference anyway, if we ever got to that point.

November 26

No word on the UN resolution. It was really wearing on me. I wasn't sleeping well worrying about it. I usually went to sleep easily from drinking enough wine, but I woke up early in the morning and slept intermittently the rest of the night. I had a headache that morning, probably from too much wine.

Even if I end my life here like this, I know I've done more things and been blessed more than any other man I know of. Not bad for half a life, eh?

November 28

I thought two guys in the compound were getting out because of their Arab background. I sent a letter with one, the one who has been selling military arms. How many letters had I sent by others who had departed? How many had gotten to Shirley?

November 30

The UN resolution 678 finally passed. The vote authorized the use of force against Iraq to uphold and implement the previous resolutions to restore Kuwait and establish peace in the area. It was now clear there would be a war over the Iraqi occupation, and I was right in the middle of it. How oddly elated we felt when we knew we were going to be in a war.

I tried to work through whether to ask Shirley to go to Iraq and Saddam Hussein to beg for my release. I wanted so badly to make it home, but I didn't want to bring her into danger. I thought we were going to get out of the mess, but the timing was uncertain. Now we had the date of January 15 as the probable beginning of the battle.

I finally got the paperwork that worried me from the State Department, for all the good it might do. But it was a mental relief.

With the date of January 15, it was less likely we would abandon the embassy and go to Baghdad. We might lose communication, but we had enough food and water to make it to January 15 and beyond. So it was the war option for us. Maybe we would get to see some real fighting.

December 1

Many here on the compound were ill with some kind of virus with headache, fever, and odd complaints. I hadn't caught it yet. It wasn't anything serious, but we weren't in any situation to handle anything. At that point, we didn't want to give up anybody to the Iraqis.

Another strange occurrence: the Iraqis brought fruit, vegetables, and soft drinks. We didn't know what to make of that gesture. Some on the compound thought we shouldn't accept any gifts from them. Was it a message of some kind? The ambassador and the DCM felt it had diplomatic significance, and we accepted the gifts. I hadn't had any kind of Coke drink for months, and I relished the chance. The soft drinks had no place to cool so they were put in the little wading pool under the tent, a minimalist attempt at lowering their temperature. Perhaps they made it down to as low as eighty degrees.

I wanted to talk to Shirley about her coming over to Iraq. There was no way to communicate accurately by notes passed back and forth. We heard many wives had come to Baghdad to beg Saddam for the release of their men, and some had met with success. None of the wives had been detained. But all this was secondhand information, and we had no way to assess the risk.

JIM AND SHIRLEY CARROLL

Maurice still hoped he might get out in a few days on a clergy pass. It has been delayed repeatedly, and it was clear the issue was wearing on him.

December 2

Everything was in order for some kind of conclusion. The UN resolution for military force was in place, the troops were getting in position; maybe the US population was getting behind the war plan. In order for this to work and have a chance of getting us out, the plan had to proceed. There was no way for either side to disengage. We couldn't look at all the awful Iraqi acts against civilians and then walk away. How selfish we all were as we languished in the embassy. We wanted war, war that would result in the deaths of many innocent Iraqi soldiers.

December 3

I knew meetings were in progress about the deadline. We kept thinking Saddam would come up with another way to avoid the issue and slip along in the status quo. He had been clever so far. We knew he couldn't be trusted. As we get closer to war, the risks of some unexpected event rose. Perhaps they would come in and take us as prisoners.

December 4

I wrote a letter to Shirley in hopes Maurice or someone else might be leaving to take it with them. Maurice's frustration rose. The possibility of getting out but not actually being released was wearing thin on him.

The letter I prepared to go with Maurice was still unclear about my wishes. If Shirley came, she might not have any access to me here in the embassy. At that point I was still not an official "human shield." I didn't want her to come alone. If there were other wives, then it might be useful and perhaps safer. And war could start any time. I knew so little of the facts that I couldn't really assess the situation. I just lacked the moral courage to say, "Don't come," because it might work for my release.

The schedule for the war, if there was one, depended on the US acting in the next few months. If they didn't, then they would best wait until fall when the temperature moderated. The heat itself was a huge enemy for troops and equipment. Even the ships in the Gulf had trouble with their cooling systems in the warm Gulf summer water.

Chapter 22

Shirley to the Rescue

Shirley

Word filtered out from the hostage wives' community that Saddam Hussein planned to release some of the hostages if their wives would come to Iraq and ask for their freedom. Of course I thought I would go and get Jim. I had been given various items of clothing and I took these to the cleaners and prepared to get ready to go to Iraq. I secured money from any source that I could and prayed about what the Lord would have me to do. The children, of course, were my main concern. What if I did not return and the children were left with nobody? I knew that John could come home for a week or so while I was gone. However, a twenty-one-year-old boy couldn't handle all the problems of raising six children and providing not only their financial support but also their care. I went to the church elders to see if there was a possibility that they could be responsible for the children's care. We had no family who would be able to take care of the children.

JIM AND SHIRLEY CARROLL

The church elders said I couldn't go and that they couldn't be held responsible for all the children.

I ended up involved with the group of wives whose husbands had been held hostage in Lebanon for years. They joined the protest to get the Kuwait hostages released. I couldn't integrate myself into their thinking. They were bitter and full of hate for their husbands' captors and who could blame them? But I wasn't bitter. The Lord had protected me from any anger against Saddam. Others wondered why it was absent, but it was missing from my thoughts. All I wanted was Jimmy out.

Even without the permission of the church elders, I still had plans to go. I knew Jimmy wanted me to come and do anything I could to see to it that he would be released. But on the other hand I wanted to follow the direction of those over me as spiritually as were the elders. I continued to seek God's guidance and his wisdom in the whole situation. I wrote the following letter.

> Dear Saddam Hussein,
>
> My husband, Jim Carroll, is in the American embassy in Kuwait. As a family man, he has been father to our seven children and husband to me. We have lived in Kuwait since August 1988. Jim wanted to use the skill God had given him in medicine to treat Arab children and to train Arab doctors in the field of pediatric medicine. In the summer of 1990 we had returned to the United States for three months, and Jim had already gone back to Kuwait by August 2, 1990. The children and I were going to go back to Kuwait on August 23, 1990. Without Jim, I am alone here in the US responsible for our seven children.
>
> I plead with you to grant him an exit visa so that he could be allowed to return to our children and me. I have enclosed a recent picture of our children. Thank you for your understanding and concern for us.
>
> Sincerely,
> Shirley Carroll

FAITH IN CRISIS

I still knew I would go anyway unless God put a stop to it. It seemed like the perfect timing to go over Christmas break when John would be at home.

Now the question was what to do about Christmas. I couldn't stand to think people would be bringing in a Christmas tree and everything else that went with it, so I went to the Christmas tree lot with all of our children. "I have only ten dollars. What kind of tree can I get for ten dollars?" Not knowing who we were at that moment, the newspaper printed our picture in the newspaper bargaining for our low-cost Christmas tree, just another of God's gifts. We brought the tree home and decorated with streamers the children made. Our Christmas tree decorations were in Kuwait.

I still had every intention of going to Iraq. I thought my plan to go during John's Christmas vacation was just the right thing. My big problem was that I didn't have a visa, and I didn't know what I was going to do about this. The Iraqis wouldn't give me a visa because they said Jimmy was not a "guest" of Iraq. I was confident God would work out this minor detail.

Chapter 23

Release and Reception

December 6 – Jim

I kept waking up much too early, too early to get out of bed. I wasn't optimistic, and my predictions have been correct just about every time. In the early morning dark, too early to roll out of bed, every possibility seemed terrible.

But this was a peculiar, unique day. I was on guard duty in the afternoon at the rear guard post and Benny and I were sitting, sweating and complaining in the concrete room with no ventilation. Lena, who had hidden out in the Shuwaikh university apartments with her husband, called. "Jim, get ready for this. The news announced that all Westerners can leave Iraq." How quickly God can turn around the worst of situations. Perhaps this was a foretaste of His coming again in glory. We got excited, our spirits jumped, but were unsure whether to believe Saddam. We tried to protect ourselves against another disappointment. We wanted to prepare for the worst.

JIM AND SHIRLEY CARROLL

We were encouraged because the embassy staff took it seriously. Barbara worked on trying to arrange a flight out of Kuwait. We all felt it was premature, but we knew the Iraqis well enough to know we had to push. The Iraq national assembly had not voted on whether or not to let us go, but everyone considered their action a rubber stamp. We feared some detail would mess up the whole thing. We leaned on the hopes and defended our expectations against another disappointment.

December 8

The spirit of hopefulness began to rise, but plans for the exit weren't formulated yet. The details suddenly became overwhelming, and the Iraqis didn't make it easy for us. We had been told we were leaving but we didn't really believe it. At every point where the Iraqis were involved there were problems. The several Arab Americans who had already gotten out of the embassy were held up in Baghdad even though the Iraqis promised them exit visas. I was frustrated with the lack of clarity about the exit plan. Maurice had been unusually upset about his lack of progress on the clergy issue. I didn't blame him, and I was afraid the same pattern would bleed over on to the rest of us as we hoped to get out. When would the exit be arranged?

December 9

The exit plan came together and we had what we believed to be a definite plan. The Iraqis would put us in a bus and take us to the airport. Apparently Saddam had lost interest in us. We speculated he thought if he let the Westerners go, then the Western allies would lose interest in the fight. We all got ready with the one bag we were allowed to take. I made strategic choices—family pictures, important knickknacks, several cans of tuna as souvenirs, now referred to as manna, the shell casings I found in

FAITH IN CRISIS

front of my house, and a couple of sweaters I had procured from the Marine barracks. I wanted to be prepared if we were diverted to northern Iraq.

The Iraqis arrived with vans. This time the Republican Guard showed up, replacing the worn-out conscripts. They were a bit scarier with their neat uniforms, shoulder epaulets, and strikingly better posture. There was uncertainty still. The Iraqis didn't yet have the orders to let us go. At his own risk and without permission of the Iraqis, the ambassador hurried across the street to see the Iraqi commander at the International Hotel, and then we were allowed to board the vans. Howell and several other diplomats stayed behind to pick up any stragglers.

We were driven out to an airport I was not acquainted with, which turned out to be Ali Al-Saleem Kuwait Air Force Base. We were then piled into a building that looked like an airport hangar, and the large doors were shut and locked. It was easy to conjure up the image of our being gassed in the building. Or were they just concerned we were going to escape from our release? A while later they came to get us and we were taken to the Iraqi 727 plane to Baghdad. We were not going on a direct flight to the US, which for me was an unanticipated detour. All along the way home my mind was in confusion—elation alternating with abject confusion.

Upon arrival in Baghdad at Saddam Hussein International Airport we had to get our exit visas. I was worried because I didn't have a passport, just a stamped paper issued by the embassy. Others before me passed through emigration, and I saw their passports were stamped for exit. I had no passport, and I was concerned about the different appearance of my paperwork. I hung back to scope out the situation, and once again the coward in me emerged. I knew Benny had the same problem I did, so I ducked behind him in line in order to let him solve the problem for me. When he went through the desk, he was stopped, and the attendant looked confused. One of the Baghdad US diplomatic staff came out and rescued Benny. I was next, and the problem had been solved.

We proceeded through the crowd, lined with news personnel and photographers from US and British stations and newspapers. Why were all these newspeople here when we were still hostages? Then we were presented with our tickets. It wasn't clear if we had assigned seats, and I didn't want to get on the plane last and find I had no seat. The departing Americans, more than 200, were made up of not only the embassy group but also those who had been holed up in various locations in Kuwait and those who had been official "human shields."

Would there be enough seats for all? But when the Iraqi Air flight for Frankfort was called, I didn't want to push to the front of the line. I ended up in the middle, a safe position. There were indeed enough seats.

The crowd on the plane was rowdy, and I was concerned. Almost all were men, and the Iraqis had cooped them up for months. They were angry and some were drunk, and I later learned others had concealed weapons. The Iraqi stewardesses were harassed almost from the beginning. I was concerned the pilot might turn the plane around and head back to Baghdad. Calmer words prevailed, and the men were settled down.

There was a joint sigh and shouts of relief when we left Iraqi airspace.

The rest of the flight was uneventful until we got to Frankfort. The Iraqi pilot descended into the airport and, just before touching down, he accelerated the 747 up from the runway. What was he doing? Was this planned? Or was there something wrong with the plane? Apparently he wasn't accustomed to the Frankfort airfield and overshot the runway. He went around quickly and made the landing.

We checked in at the Frankfort airport hotel, courtesy of the State Department, and all private rooms.

FAITH IN CRISIS

Joe came down to my room to make a phone call. I still had a credit card that was working for calls.

After he left I tried to reach Shirley. I called several times. No answer. My fear was that, due to the ambiguity of my communications with her, she was off to Baghdad to see Saddam and beg for my release. What a potential mess. I was almost home and now she was gone.

I wanted to reach friends in Augusta, but of course I had no phone numbers. I thought of our friends with the distinctive names and came up with "Volpitto" and asked for their number. Barbara answered. She didn't know where Shirley was. Perhaps she had come to meet me at Andrews Air Force Base. She had no knowledge of her going to Baghdad. I drifted to sleep wondering where she was.

The next morning breakfast was marvelous. The buffet contained all kinds of meats and other items we hadn't gotten for months.

Later we boarded the US flight to Andrews Air Force Base. The long flight over the Atlantic left me lots of time to worry. Would she be there? And if she wasn't, then what? How would I learn where she was?

Finally we landed and got off the plane via a high ladder rolled up to it. The base was overflowing with press and photographers plus others. We were herded into a large auditorium, and the first familiar voice I heard was Ruth's. Shirley was there, and she had brought all the kids except John who was at college. The relief drenched me. All the frustration and fear that had plagued me for months dissipated in a flash. I had thought I might never see my family again on this earth, and here they were hugging me.

Any remaining worries about Romans 8:28 evaporated. Jesus was as real as ever. He never changed, but I did. And I knew if the episode had ended differently, that Romans 8:28 would still be true.

JIM AND SHIRLEY CARROLL

We were all supposed to adjourn to a hotel for a "debriefing." I'd had enough of governments, any government, and we got into the borrowed station wagon and headed off. No debriefing for me.

December 9—Shirley

All the State Department rep could tell me was that some Americans had been sent to a Baghdad, then on to Frankfort, and were to arrive at Andrews Air Force Base airport in Washington, DC. They said they thought a doctor was among those being released, but they did not know who it was. I asked the church if I could drive the loaned car to Washington, DC. They said I could. The plane was to arrive Sunday morning. The children and I all piled into the car and headed for Washington, DC. Several friends from the church and community called to tell me what a mistake I was making to take the children for such an uncertainty, but I had great peace that I was doing the right thing. Jim was going to be there. As a family we had experienced great joy and praise to God for His continued faithfulness to each of us. He would continue to be faithful.

A friend made one final phone call. "Shirley, don't take the children all the way up there when you don't even know if Jim will be on the plane." I knew he would be on the plane, and the children believed me. I was so sure Jim would make it on the plane that I took the children there by car against the advice of everyone who knew I was going.

We arrived at the confusion of Andrews Air Force Base with all the reporters, cameras, tons of families with children of all sizes. The children and I followed everyone into a large open room where several hundred people were milling around, finding each other and embracing. I didn't see Jimmy. Nearly an hour went by and it looked like everyone had entered. He wasn't there. How could this be? Had I tricked myself into being certain he was coming

FAITH IN CRISIS

even though there had been no confirmation, just "a doctor on the plane?" And there I was with six children all watching the door to the building, the children I had promised their dad would be coming. For too long a moment I was mad at God for assuring me Jimmy would be there. My heart was pounding, and I was trying not to cry in front of the kids.

Then Ruth said, "There's Dad!" and she ran to him. He had been one of the last to get off the plane. God kept His "promise," the one He put in my heart.

I was elated, but I was also concerned. What had he been through? Would he have the effects many other hostages have had after such an experience—depression, anger, and resentment? But there was only happiness. Jimmy had no obvious emotional scars, and he looked well physically. The hugging continued for minutes with the children each wanting their own individual attention from dad. Jimmy spread the love around among them. All the foregoing apprehension, worry, and tension flew away. The event swept over me in a wave, and I was enveloped. There were no emotions that were sufficient. The Lord was sufficient, and He had carried us through the months.

But after hugging us all and walking back to the car, Jimmy began to talk about another matter. "Have you seen what's happening to all those Romanian kids?" Romania had just been freed in the last year from the long, torturous reign of Nicolae Ceausescu. Many children born in the regime had ended up without parents and no way to survive. "Do you think we could adopt one of those kids?"

At that moment I knew he was fine.

We tried the Romanian route of adoption but there were too many complications. No one knew who the parents of the children were, and there was no way to get a legal adoption.

We took the Korean path again and ended up with Elizabeth, a little girl with one arm and a big heart. But that's another story.

Epilogue

I returned to Kuwait in the spring. Guns had taken over Kuwait City. Burned out Iraqi tanks were still dug in all over the town center. Residents were determined not to tolerate such subjugation by outsiders again. They would defend themselves the next time. The cab driver showed me the AK-47 in his trunk. He was clear. "Everyone has one now."

Our home had been looted, either by the Iraqis or Kuwaitis desperate for whatever they could garner for survival. Our wedding pictures, which we had taken with us to Kuwait, were gone. Why would they want our wedding photos?

I went downtown to the embassy where they were helpful in selling the vehicle I had driven into the compound in August of the prior year. The embassy had remained intact after our departure with no incursion by the Iraqis. Our own overzealous Special Forces had done the only damage as they swarmed into the city.

My return to the hospital revealed that my friend, Faisal, with his Palestinian background, had been removed from the university faculty as a potential traitor, even though he had remained faithfully to care for the children.

But the greatest disappointment was Rania. The doctors and the hospital social worker were anxious to inform me about her end. The stories varied. One said she was brought to the hospital with severe dehydration and malnutrition. Another related she was discovered beaten to death in a closet in the family's apartment. But the conclusion was the same: Rania was dead. In my mind the Iraqis killed her. We could have helped had we been able to remain in Kuwait.

The situation in Kuwait was not suitable for us to return, and in Augusta the university generously returned my former job.

Shirley says I still suffer from posttraumatic stress disorder (PTSD), an accusation I adamantly deny. My bad dreams mean nothing, and the fact she has to depart for her own protection to the living room sofa when I start flailing about has no significance.

The Lord has continued to bless us. In the year after my return we adopted little Elizabeth from Korea, our eighth. First Presbyterian Church in Augusta has continued as our refuge, and they have allowed us to serve locally. We have thirteen (almost fourteen) grandchildren.

Shirley and I agree: the Lord is good in all things.

The Authors

The only child of older parents, Jim spent his childhood in the small town of Eminence, Kentucky. "I could ride my bike everywhere, go fishing anywhere. It was 'A River Runs Through It' childhood." Following the family move to Louisville for better schooling, Jim began college after his high school junior year, finished college in two years, and started medical school at twenty. After a stint in the Navy, a career in medical research carried him from the University of Colorado to Washington University in St. Louis and finally to the Medical College of Georgia, where he was Chief of Child Neurology.

In the 1980's, Jim sensed a call to Christian foreign missions. The family charged off to Kuwait where this story of crisis ensued. Jim is "retired" but continues with patient care and stem cell research. He hopes to make things better for brain-injured babies through application of new treatments with stem cells. When he has time, Jim roams the North Georgia mountains in spring and summer in search of the rainbow trout and the pine forests of South Georgia in the fall and winter in pursuit of his target, the white tail deer. And in both, there is fellowship with his sons and family. He is an elder in First Presbyterian Church (PCA), Augusta, Georgia.

JIM AND SHIRLEY CARROLL

Shirley was born in Louisville, Kentucky. Her grandmother, who exemplified true Christian living, brought her up. After completing college and her Masters' degree in sociology, she began a career in social work. She had no intention of marriage, but Jim swept her off her feet. They decided to get married after five weeks. Shirley served as a community organizer for four local churches and a community house working to minister to the needs of an inner city changing neighborhood. After dodging bullets in the downtown Louisville church during the riots of 1968, Shirley and Jim departed for Washington, DC, and Jim's two years in the navy. It was time for a family.

After eight children and fourteen grandchildren, there is no retirement for Shirley. Her joy is devoting time to Jim, her children, and grandchildren. She also loves spending time with other women and seeking mutual growth in the Lord.